How To F[...] Your O[...]n Corporation Without A Lawyer For Under $75.00

Ted Nicholas

UPSTART PUBLISHING COMPANY

Specializing in Small Business Publishing
a division of Dearborn Publishing Group, Inc.

This publication is designed to provide accurate and authoritative information in regard to the subject matter covered. It is sold with the understanding that the publisher is not engaged in rendering legal, accounting or other professional service. If legal advice or other expert assistance is required, the services of a competent professional person should be sought.

Hard Cover Printings:
©1972 by Ted Nicholas
First Printing January 1973
Second Printing May 1973
Third Printing December 1973
Fourth Printing December 1973
Fifth Printing (Revised April 1974) ©1974 by Ted Nicholas
Sixth Printing (Revised September 1975) ©1975 by Ted Nicholas
Seventh Printing (Revised September 1976) ©1976 by Ted Nicholas
Eighth Printing (March 1977) ©1977 by Ted Nicholas
Ninth Printing (Revised November 1977) ©1977 by Ted Nicholas
Tenth Printing (December 1977) ©1977 by Ted Nicholas
Eleventh Printing (April 1978) ©1978 by Ted Nicholas
Twelfth Printing (July 1978) Special Edition ©1978 by Ted Nicholas
Thirteenth Printing (Revised April 1979) ©1979 by Ted Nicholas
Fourteenth Printing ©1980 by Ted Nicholas
Fifteenth Printing ©1980 by Ted Nicholas
Sixteenth Printing ©1981 by Ted Nicholas
Seventeenth Printing ©1981 by Ted Nicholas

Eighteenth Printing (Revised September 1981)
©1981 by Ted Nicholas
Fifteen Quality Paperback Printings 1977–1992
(Revised January 1982) ©1982 by Ted Nicholas
(Revised February 1983) ©1983 by Ted Nicholas
(Revised November 1983) ©1983 by Ted Nicholas
(Revised February 1984) ©1984 by Ted Nicholas
(Revised February 1985) ©1985 by Ted Nicholas
(Revised September 1985) ©1985 by Ted Nicholas
(Revised May 1986) ©1986 by Ted Nicholas
(Revised November 1986) ©1986 by Ted Nicholas
(Revised May 1987) ©1987 by Ted Nicholas
(Revised March 1989) ©1989 by Ted Nicholas
(Revised February 1990) ©1990 by Ted Nicholas
(Revised February 1991) ©1991 by Ted Nicholas
(Revised November 1991) ©1991 by Ted Nicholas
(Revised March 1992) ©1992 by Ted Nicholas
(Revised May 1996) ©1996 by Ted Nicholas

Published by Upstart Publishing Company,
a division of Dearborn Publishing Group, Inc.

Printed in the United States of America

96 97 98 10 9 8 7 6 5 4 3 2 1

Library of Congress Cataloging-in-Publication Data

Nicholas, Ted, 1934-
    How to form your own corporation without a lawyer for under $75.00/
Ted Nicholas.—25th anniversary ed.
        p. cm.
    Includes index.
    ISBN 1-57410-023-8 (paper)
1. Incorporation—Delaware—Popular works. I. Title.
KFD213.Z9N5 1996
346.751'06622—dc20   96-284
[347.5106622]   CIP

For mail orders, write Nicholas Direct, Inc., 1511 Gulf Blvd., P. O. Box 877, Indian Rocks Beach, FL 34635

DEDICATION

To businessmen and women who have successfully incorporated by using this book and to all of you budding entrepreneurs who will soon be incorporating your dream business.

ACKNOWLEDGMENTS

I'd like to thank my friend, Sylvan N. Levy, Jr., for his useful suggestions after spending many hours reviewing the manuscript.

Additionally, the entire staff of Upstart Publishing Company as well as reviewer Robert Friedman have been of enormous assistance in the preparation of this book.

MORE ACKNOWLEDGMENTS

In connection with this writing, special acknowledgment is given the Corporation Department, Secretary of State's office in Dover, Delaware, and its capable staff.

In particular, I deeply appreciate the efforts of the Assistant Secretary of State, Richard H. Caldwell, for his personal assistance and helpful comments in reviewing this book.

Since the first printing of the hardcover edition in January 1973, Robert Reed, Secretary of State appointed by Governor Sherman Tribbitt, Grover Biddle, the Assistant Secretary of State, and Marie Shultie, Director, Corporation Department, and her staff have been of enormous assistance in helping to process smoothly and efficiently the large volume of new corporations from all over the world that have been formed as a result of this book.

At the time of this printing, the present Secretary of State, Edward J. Freel, appointed by Governor Thomas Carper, continues with the fine work that historically has been done by the Corporation Department.

T.N.

A BRIEF HISTORY OF THE CORPORATION

Most of American law has its origin in England. The corporation as a legal entity under English law dates back to the late fourteenth century. In the early 1600s, again in England, a number of joint stock associations were formed in an attempt to gain the same advantages as chartered corporations. In all contractual dealings, these companies were able to offer their shareholders liability protection. As a result, investors in such companies were in a more favorable position than partners whose liabilities for partnership debts were unlimited.

Corporations have been a part of North America's history for over 300 years. The Massachusetts Bay Company was chartered in 1629 by Charles I of England. Its purpose was to colonize the area near Massachusetts Bay. In 1630, it founded the city of Boston. The Hudson Bay Company of Canada was chartered in 1670 and continues to operate trading posts there today.

During the early stages of the American Republic, it took a special act of a state legislature to grant a corporate charter to a business enterprise. The first state to permit incorporation under a general law was New York in 1811. By 1900, nearly all the states had constitutional provisions forbidding the granting of corporate charters by legislators.

Until the the Delaware General Corporation Law was adopted in 1899, Delaware too had granted corporate charters by an act of the legislature. Delaware was the pioneer state in creating an attractive climate for free enterprise. Many of the corporations begun during America's great industrial revolution of the 1800s were chartered in Delaware. Its friendly and accommodating atmosphere toward business enterprises still exists. Low taxes, fast service, simplified requirements and the Court of Chancery, the only separate business court system in the United States, combine to attract both small one-person corporations and large corporations to Delaware. One-third of the companies listed on the American and New York Stock Exchanges are chartered in Delaware.

Corporations in America in the early stages were burdened with sharp restrictions on longevity and size. Terms were fixed to a specific number of years, 20 to 50 years being common. There were also ceilings on authorized capital. These and other limits were abandoned over time.

In the 1700s corporations carried on a large part of world commerce. By the late 1800s corporations had multiplied enormously. Nearly every business owner that required capital or a union of large numbers of people, or desired limited liability, incorporated. The wealth and business holdings in the country to a great extent were and still are controlled by them.

At present the states compete with each other to attract business. Some are more aggressive than others, which creates a healthy atmosphere. Many have attempted to model sections of their law on the General Corporation Law of Delaware. However, while there are some similarities, no state has been successful in achieving all of Delaware's benefits.

Today, more than 2 million active corporations exist. About 800,000 of these have elected to be taxed like partnerships. According to *The Wall Street Journal,* more than 50,000 new corporations are formed each month in North America. With the publication of this revised 25th anniversary edition, this book will be used by a growing number of them—500 to 600 each month, or nearly 2 percent of all the corporations formed each month in the United States.

CONTENTS

Definition: A corporation is an entity created through the filing by one or more individuals of a document known as *articles of incorporation* or *certificate of incorporation* with a state agency known as the Corporation Department. This entity is recognized by law as a separate "person" existing in reality with limited liability, a separate tax status, the right to sue and be sued, the option of selling shares and the capacity of succession.

"For many years, even decades, the Delaware General Corporation Law has been the pacesetter for American corporation statutes. Indeed, viewed realistically, Delaware Corporation Law is national corporation law."

"The fact is that states cannot effectively exert controls and restrictions even over enterprises organized under their own corporation statutes. If they attempt to do so, enterprises merely incorporate in some other state with a more 'liberal' statute since the federal system permits individuals to incorporate wherever they wish in order to do business on a local, state, national, or international level."

> From *The Delaware General Corporation Law*
> by Ernest L. Folk III, Professor of Law,
> University of Virginia, and published for
> Corporation Service Company by
> Little, Brown and Company, Inc.
> 34 Beacon Street
> Boston, MA 02106

"Anyone may so arrange his affairs that his taxes shall be as low as possible; he is not bound to choose that pattern which will best pay the Treasury; there is not even a patriotic duty to increase one's taxes."

> Judge Learned Hand

PREFACE

This printing is a milestone in the many previous editions of this book. This printing marks the 25th anniversary edition. A full revision and updating has been done. More than 1 million copies are now in print. This edition therefore becomes most significant. People from all 50 states and several thousand readers from other parts of the world have already used this material to form corporations.

This book enables the reader to incorporate at the lowest possible cost. The necessary forms are in tear-out type complete with instructions.

The author is the founder of The Company Corporation. This corporation provides various low-cost services to persons who form a corporation (See Section VIII).

Lawyers' fees for incorporating range from $300 to $3,000 or more. The system enables anyone in the United States to form a corporation without a lawyer at the lowest possible cost, and includes other money-saving and tax-saving ideas.

A little-known fact is that an individual can legally incorporate in many states without the services of a lawyer. Lawyers provide important professional services to their clients. However, incorporation is a relatively simple task that does not require professional services. Forming a corporation usually involves minimum legal fees of at least $300.

Before this book was written, it was difficult for an individual to incorporate without a lawyer because there was no such publication on the subject written in everyday English. In addition, companies that assist individuals in forming a corporation work only through lawyers who prepare the corporate documents. Legal fees for incorporation prior to this book were almost completely unavoidable.

Delaware is emphasized as the state in which to incorporate. Regardless of where a person lives or has a business, this book enables a person to incorporate and take advantage of Delaware's corporate laws. In Delaware, anyone can form a corporation so long as he or she completes the forms provided for that purpose. You can find the reason for this in Section II. Delaware is the state of incorporation for over 200,000 corporations that range from small one-person operations to the largest in the United States. Because of the advantages to corporations of Delaware's corporate laws, more than one-third of all corporations listed on the American and New York Stock Exchanges are Delaware corporations. This is a much higher percentage than any other state.

The biggest percentage of the corporations formed in Delaware are headquartered in other states. The individuals who own these corporations almost never visit the state.

More than 30 companies act as a *registered agent* and provide such services as a Delaware mailing address for the corporations formed in Delaware.

In most cases, the needs of an individual or company that wishes to incorporate involve a simple corporate structure. The goal of this book is directed toward the simplest and lowest-cost method of forming a corporation. A person with a business of any type or size who wishes to incorporate and conduct business anywhere in the United States can beneficially utilize the elements in this book.

With this edition, many thousands of new corporations have been formed by using this book.

Prices and fees quoted in this book may be increased without notice by the various states and other bodies, and should be used only as a guide.

ADVANTAGES AND DISADVANTAGES OF INCORPORATING

SECTION I

Before you decide whether to incorporate, review other alternatives.

You can choose from two other fundamental ways to operate a business—individual proprietorship and general partnership. (**Note:** The comparisons in Section I apply only to general partnerships, not to limited partnerships or limited liability partnerships.) Both have similar advantages and disadvantages. The main advantage is that they are slightly less expensive to start as there are no incorporating fees. They are also a bit less formal.

In a corporation, periodic meetings and minutes of meetings should be kept. This is a simple, routine task. (See Section XXIII.)

ADVANTAGES OF GENERAL PARTNERSHIPS AND PROPRIETORSHIPS:

1. The cost to organize is lower because there are no incorporating fees.
2. Record keeping is less formal.
3. The owners file one tax return.
4. Owners can deduct losses that might be incurred during the early life of a business from other personal income.
5. The limit of tax-deductible contributions to Keogh-type pension and profit-sharing plans has been increased to the smaller of 25 percent of the participants' contributions or $30,000. This has reduced the tax advantage of benefit plans previously available to a corporation.
6. Profits of a partnership, unlike dividends paid by a corporation, are not subject to a second federal income tax when distributed to the owners. However, whether this is a tax benefit depends on certain other factors, namely:
   a. The individual tax brackets of the owners as compared with that of the corporation
   b. The extent to which double taxation of earnings of the corporation is eliminated by deductible salaries paid to owners and by retention of earnings in surplus
   c. Deductions for fringe benefits that are unavailable in partnerships but fully deductible in corporations
   d. The availability of the S corporation, which offers the tax advantages of a partnership and the protection of a corporation

SOME DISADVANTAGES OF PROPRIETORSHIPS AND GENERAL PARTNERSHIPS:

1. There is unlimited personal liability. The owners are personally liable for all debts and judgments against the business, including liability in case of failure or other disaster.
2. In a partnership, each member can bind the other so that one partner can cause the other to be personally liable.
3. If the owner(s) dies or becomes incapacitated, the business often comes to a standstill.
4. The owner(s) does not have the full tax benefits of tax-deductible fringe benefit plans, including pension and profit sharing that are available to a corporation.

ADVANTAGES OF INCORPORATING:

1.   The personal liability of the founders is limited to the amount of money put into the corporation (with the exception of unpaid taxes).

2.   If a business owner wishes to raise capital, a corporation is more attractive to investors, who can purchase shares of stock in it for raising capital.

3.   A corporation does not pay tax on monies it receives in exchange for its stock.

4.   Many more tax options are available to corporations than to proprietorships or partnerships. One can set up pension, profit-sharing, and stock option plans that are favorable to the owners of the corporation.

5.   A corporation can be continued more easily in the event of the death of its owners or principals.

6.   Shares of a corporation can easily be distributed to family members.

7.   The owners (shareholders) of a corporation that is discontinued because it is unsuccessful can have all the advantages of being incorporated, yet be able to deduct from personal income up to $50,000 on an individual tax return or $100,000 on a joint return of the amount that was invested in the corporation. (See Section XVII.)

8.   The owner(s), that is, shareholders, of a corporation can operate with all the advantages of a corporation, yet be taxed at personal income tax rates if this option provides a tax advantage. (See Section XVIII.)

9.   Owners can quickly transfer their ownership interest represented by shares of stock without the corporation's dissolving.

10.   The corporation's capital can be expanded by issuing and selling additional shares of stock.

11.   Shares of stock can be used for estate and family planning.

12.   The corporation can ease the tax burden of its shareholders by accumulating its earnings if the accumulation is not unreasonable and is for a business purpose.

13.   A corporation is a legal "being," separate and apart from its owner(s) (shareholders). It can sue and be sued and can enter into contracts.

14.   A corporation may own shares in another corporation and receive dividends, 80 percent of which are tax free.

15.   A corporation's federal income tax rates may be lower than the owner's individual tax rates, especially for a company with taxable income in the $28,000 to $100,000 range. As of this printing, income tax rates on companies are as follows:

Taxable Income	Rate of Tax
Up to $50,000	15%
$50,000–$75,000	$7,500 plus 25% of the amount over $75,000
$75,000–$100,000	$13,750 plus 34% of the amount over $75,000
$100,000–$335,000	$22,250 plus 39% of the amount over $100,000
$335,000–$10,000,000	$113,900 plus 34% of the amount over $335,000
$10,000,000–$15,000,000	$3,400,000 plus 35% of the amount over $10,000,000
$15,000,000–$18,333,333	$5,150,000 plus 38% of the amount over $15,000,000
Over $18,333,333	35%

DISADVANTAGES OF INCORPORATING:

1.   The owners of a corporation file two tax returns, individual and corporate, which may require added time and accounting expense. (The owner of a proprietorship files one return; a member of a partnership files only one return, and the partnership files an information return.)

2.   If the net taxable income of a business is substantial (i.e., $75,000 or more), there may not be tax advantages. Again, the S corporation option allows corporate income to be treated as the income of the individual owners, and the income is taxed at their individual rates, not at corporate rates. Furthermore, in businesses where there is personal liability on the part of the owners, it may be desirable to incorporate even if the income is modest.

3.   Maintaining corporate records may require added time. (See corporate forms, Section XXIII.)

4.   If debt financing is obtained by a corporation (i.e., a loan from a bank), the fund source may require the personal guarantee by the owner(s), thereby eliminating the limited-liability advantage of a corporation, at least to the extent of the loan. But as the business continues to operate and demonstrates a sound financial history, many lenders will accept a corporation's promise to pay without requiring its owners to guarantee payment.

     NOTE: Probably the biggest single disadvantage to incorporating prior to the publication of this book was the high initial cost.

REASONS FOR INCORPORATING IN DELAWARE

SECTION II

THE ADVANTAGES OF INCORPORATING IN DELAWARE INCLUDE THE FOLLOWING:

1.   There is *no* minimum capital requirement. A corporation can be organized with zero capital, if desired. Several states require that a corporation have at least $1,000 in capital.

2.   *One* person can hold the offices of president, treasurer, and secretary, and be the entire board of directors. Many states require at least three officers and/or directors. Therefore, there is no need to bring other persons into a Delaware corporation if the owner(s) does not desire it.

3.   An established body of law governs corporations that have been tested in the Delaware courts over the years. There is therefore a high degree of predictability of the outcome of any legal proceedings in Delaware based on past history and experience. This can be meaningful to investors in a corporation. The Court of Chancery in Delaware is the only separate business court system in the United States, and it has a long record of promanagement decisions.

4.   There is no corporate income tax for any corporations that are formed in Delaware but do not do business in the state.

5.   The franchise tax on corporations compares favorably with that in any other state.

6.   Shares of stock owned by a person outside the state are not subject to any Delaware taxes.

7.   A person can operate as the owner of a Delaware corporation anonymously if desired. (See Section XVI.)

8.   One can form a corporation by mail and never visit the state, even to conduct annual meetings. Meetings can be held anywhere at the option of the directors.

9.   The Delaware Corporation Department welcomes new corporations and is organized to process them the same day they are received.

10. Delaware is the state friendliest to corporations because it depends on its Corporation Department as a prime source of revenue. The corporation revenue is exceeded by income taxes. The state therefore depends on attracting a high volume of corporations. It has historically kept its laws and fees relevant to corporations favorable and at a low cost.

11. There is no inheritance tax on shares of stock held by nonresidents. These shares are taxed only in the state of residence of the corporation owners.

12. Directors may fix a sales price on any stock that the corporation issues and wishes to sell.

13. Shareholders, directors, and/or committee members may act by unanimous written consent in lieu of formal meetings.

14. Directors may determine what part of the consideration received for stock is capital.

15. Corporations can pay dividends out of profits as well as from surplus.

16. Corporations can hold stocks, bonds, or securities of other corporations, real and personal property, within or without the state, without any limitation as to amount.

17. Corporations may purchase shares of their own stock and hold, sell and transfer them.

18. Corporations may conduct different kinds of business in combination. If the corporate documents filed with Delaware have the broadest type of "purpose clause" as outlined in

this book, any business activity of any kind may be conducted. More than one type of business can be conducted by the same corporation without any changes in the documents filed with the state.

19. Corporations have perpetual existence (unless specified otherwise in the Certificate of Incorporation).

20. The directors have power to make or alter bylaws.

21. Shareholder's liability is limited to stock held in the corporation (with the exception of taxes and assuming the business is conducted in a legal manner).

22. Only one person acting as the incorporator is required, whereas many states require three.

23. Directors' personal liability is either entirely eliminated or strictly limited under a new law passed in 1986 (Section 102(b)(7), Title 8 of the Delaware Code).

24. Recent legislation has provided a balance between the benefits of an unfettered market for corporate shares and the well-documented and judicially recognized need to limit abusive takeover tactics.

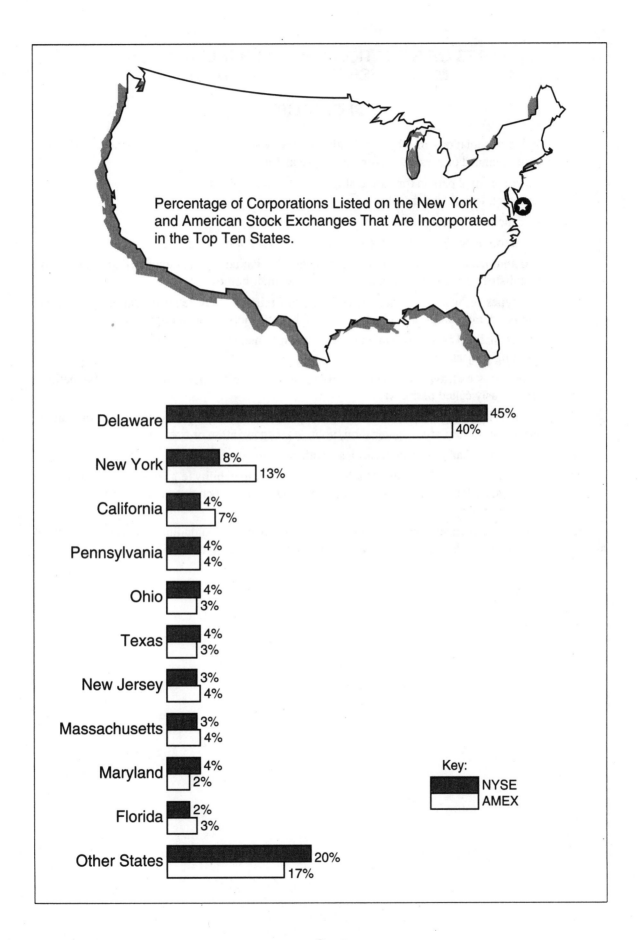

Percentage of Corporations Listed on the New York and American Stock Exchanges That Are Incorporated in the Top Ten States.

State	NYSE	AMEX
Delaware	45%	40%
New York	8%	13%
California	4%	7%
Pennsylvania	4%	4%
Ohio	4%	3%
Texas	4%	3%
New Jersey	3%	4%
Massachusetts	3%	4%
Maryland	4%	2%
Florida	2%	3%
Other States	20%	17%

Key:
NYSE
AMEX

TYPES OF SITUATIONS IN WHICH INDIVIDUALS MIGHT WISH TO INCORPORATE

SECTION III

A few examples of situations in which individuals may wish to incorporate a business activity or profession either planned or presently in operation are as follows:

1. A professional person (or partnership) such as an accountant, engineer, physician, dentist, architect, lawyer and the like

2. A franchised business owner

3. A person or company planning to conduct a private or public stock offering

4. A manufacturing service or retailing business that includes a manufacturer's representative or a distributor (many of whom operate out of their homes)

   The types of businesses include, but are not limited to, any retail operation, gas station, publisher, mail order operation, restaurant, beauty shop and loan company.

5. A personal real estate investment, such as an apartment building, store, or any commercial-building project

6. A business endeavor involving the ownership of one or more shareholders (sometimes erroneously called partners)

7. An activity or organization that is organized for nonprofit purposes, such as a foundation, association, charitable organization, volunteer organization or fire company

8. A company that invests in securities or other companies

9. A person who forms a business that creates exposure to liability (e.g., businesses that operate vehicles, perform construction work, offer food, or offer such personal services as physical training or hair care).

It often makes good sense from both a tax and personal liability standpoint for certain interests of an individual, such as a real estate investment, to be incorporated separately.

CERTIFICATE OF INCORPORATION

SECTION IV

When a Delaware corporation is formed, a certificate of incorporation is filed with the Secretary of State's office and with the Recorder of Deeds. It is also necessary to prepare minutes of the first directors' meeting, bylaws of the corporation, stock certificates and the corporate seal (forms for everything except stock certificates and the corporate seal are supplied in this book).

Any person or his or her registered agent (see Section VII) can file the Certificate of Incorporation.

An individual or his registered agent can also arrange to provide the corporation with a Delaware address. Preparation of minutes of the first directors' meeting, bylaws, stock certificates and corporate seal can be ordered and completed by the person incorporating. Minutes and bylaws in standard form can be removed from this book and used for this purpose. A complete sample specimen and blank Certificate of Incorporation are shown in Section V. Forms for bylaws and minutes are in Section XXIII.

A very important element of the certificate is the purpose clause in paragraph three. The broadest clause enabling the corporation to engage in any business activity is used in this book. No matter what businesses the corporation engages in, this clause need not be changed. The broadest powers are given to the director(s) and officer(s). The only types of corporations to which this clause does not apply are institutions, schools, insurance companies, professional corporations, and banks.

Fifteen hundred shares of stock, which is the maximum number for the minimum state fee, are used in the sample specimen. This premise takes into consideration the annual corporate franchise fee, which is only $30 for 1,500 shares. If this number of shares or any lesser number is selected initially as the number authorized by the corporation, it can easily be changed at any time if more shares are to be issued later. More shares, stock splits or a new capital structure require only a simple form to be filed with the state. A schedule showing the fees for these types of changes is available from the Secretary of State, Dover, Delaware. A Delaware registered agent can file the forms involving these changes, or they can be filed by an individual residing anywhere in the United States.

FORMING THE CORPORATION WITHOUT ENGAGING A REGISTERED AGENT

SECTION V

Any person can form a Delaware corporation. The owner(s) never has to visit the state. Annual meetings may be held anywhere.

Below is the least costly way to accomplish the incorporation. (This approach, while the least costly, does not include the benefits of the services a registered agent can provide.)

The following are the steps involved:

1. Establish a street mailing address in Delaware. This can be a private home or office. (Without engaging a registered agent's services to provide assistance, this is usually the most difficult problem to solve.) See Section VII.

2. Decide whether to form a regular corporation or close corporation. (See Section VI.) Complete the blank certificate of incorporation on the following pages, using the same format on the succeeding page. The language in this certificate has been prepared by the Secretary of State, Dover, Delaware. Be sure to fill in the name and address of one incorporator who resides in any state.

   Send two copies of this certificate to the Secretary of State, Corporation Department, Townsend Building, Dover, Delaware 19901. Include a check for $50, which is the total cost of the incorporation. (This fee breaks down as follows: $25 for filing, receiving and indexing; $15, the minimum state filing fee; and $10 for a certified copy.)

   If the corporate name you pick is not available, you will be notified. Otherwise you will receive notice of the date that your corporation has been filed.

3. When you receive one certified copy of the Certificate of Incorporation plus a receipted bill from the state, file this copy with the Recorder of Deeds' office in the county where the street mailing address of the corporation is located. There are three counties in Delaware. The addresses for the Recorder of Deeds' offices in the three counties are as follows:

   Kent County–County Courthouse, Dover, Delaware 19901

   Sussex County–Box 505, Georgetown, Delaware 19947

   New Castle County–800 French Street, Wilmington, Delaware 19801

   Enclose a check for $24* (The charge is $9 *per page* submitted with a minimum of $18 to record a one-page certificate and certification page plus a $6 document-recording fee. Conventional certificates prepared and typed on legal-size paper are from four to ten pages, costing the person filing from $42 to $96. This is the reason that all certificates of incorporation except nonstock are printed on one page and are available from The Company Corporation.)

   In some states other than Delaware, a similar incorporation procedure applies. If a reader is interested in forming a non-Delaware corporation, that person can obtain specific information by writing to the Corporation Department, Secretary of State, in any state. However, no state has all the benefits of incorporating in Delaware.

---

* *Applies to New Castle County only.*

Standard forms are provided in Section XXIII for bylaws and minutes of the first meeting.

There are also legal-stationery companies that can supply a complete kit of the above forms at a cost ranging from $65 to $90. A corporate seal and stock certificates cost $20 to $30.

The Company Corporation provides a kit that includes a corporate seal, stock certificates, forms for minutes for Section 1244 of the Internal Revenue Code (see Section VIII) for $79.95, plus $8.00 for UPS delivery.

If you prefer to engage a registered agent to act in your behalf, such services can easily be obtained. (See Section VII.)

CERTIFICATE OF INCORPORATION
of
JOHN DOE, INC.

FIRST: The name of this corporation is _(repeat name exactly as above)_
JOHN DOE, INC.

SECOND. Its registered office in the State of Delaware is to be located at _Three Christina Centre, 201 North Walnut Street_ in the City of _Wilmington,_ County of _New Castle._ The registered agent in charge thereof is _(name and address of your registered agent)_ The Company Corporation at _same as above._

THIRD: The nature of the business and the objects and purposes to be transacted, promoted and carried on are to do any or all the things herein mentioned as fully and to the same extent as natural persons might or could do, and in any part of the world, viz:

"The purpose of the corporation is to engage in any lawful act or activity for which corporations may be organized under the General Corporation Law of Delaware."

FOURTH: The amount of the total authorized capital stock of this corporation is _1,500_ _____ share of _no_ par value.

FIFTH: The name and mailing address of the incorporator is as follows:
NAME: ADDRESS:
(leave blank if using The Company Corporation as agent otherwise your name and address)

SIXTH: The powers of the incorporator are to terminate upon filing of the certificate of incorporation, and the name(s) and mailing address(es) of persons who are to serve as director(s) until the first annual meeting of shareholders or until their successors are elected and qualify are as follows:

Name and address of director(s)

John Doe, 1 Main Street, Atlantis, CA   [fill in name(s)
Jane Doe, 1 Main Street, Atlantis, CA   and address(es)]

SEVENTH: The directors shall have power to make and to alter or amend the bylaws; to fix the amount to be reserved as working capital; and to authorize and cause to be executed mortgages and liens without limit as to the amount upon the property and franchise of the corporation.

With the consent in writing, and pursuant to a vote of the holders of a majority of the capital stock issued and outstanding, the directors shall have the authority to dispose in any manner of the whole property of this corporation.

The bylaws shall determine whether and to what extent the accounts and books of this corporation, or any of them, shall be open to the inspection of the shareholders; and no shareholder shall have any right of inspecting any account or book or document of this corporation, except as conferred by the law or the bylaws, or by resolution of the shareholders.

The shareholders and directors shall have power to hold their meetings and keep the books, documents and papers of the corporation outside of the State of Delaware, at such places as may be from time to time designated by the bylaws or by resolution of the shareholders or directors, except as otherwise required by the laws of Delaware.

It is the intention that the objects, purposes and powers specified in the third paragraph hereof shall, except where otherwise specified in said paragraph, be nowise limited or restricted by reference to or inference from the terms of any other clause or paragraph in this certificate of incorporation, but that the objects, purposes and powers specified in the third paragraph and in each of the clauses or paragraphs of this charter shall be regarded as independent objects, purposes and powers.

EIGHTH: Directors of the corporation shall not be liable to either the corporation or its shareholders for monetary damages for a breach of fiduciary duties unless the breach involves: (1) a director's duty of loyalty to the corporation or its shareholders; (2) acts or omissions not in good faith or which involve intentional misconduct or a knowing violation of law; (3) liability for unlawful payments of dividends or unlawful stock purchases or redemption by the corporation; or (4) a transaction from which the director derived an improper personal benefit.

I, THE UNDERSIGNED, for the purpose of forming a corporation under the laws of the State of Delaware, do make, file and record this certificate and do certify that the facts herein are true; and I have accordingly hereunto set my hand.

DATED AT: _____

State of _____

County of _____
(leave blank unless you are incorporator)

_____
John Doe
(signature of person or officer of corporation named in fifth article)
(leave blank if using The Company Corporation)

CERTIFICATE OF INCORPORATION
of
_____

FIRST: The name of this corporation is _____

_____

SECOND: Its registered office in the State of Delaware is to be located at _____ _____ in the City of _____ County of _____ _____. The registered agent in charge thereof is _____ _____ at _____.

THIRD: The nature of the business and the objects and purposes to be transacted, promoted and carried on are to do any or all the things herein mentioned as fully and to the same extent as natural persons might or could do, and in any part of the world, viz:

"The purpose of the corporation is to engage in any lawful act or activity for which corporations may be organized under the General Corporation Law of Delaware."

FOURTH: The amount of the total authorized capital stock of this corporation is _____ _____ share of _____ par value.

FIFTH: The name and mailing address of the incorporator is as follows:

NAME: ADDRESS:

_____   _____

                                             _____

SIXTH: The powers of the incorporator are to terminate upon filing of the certificate of incorporation, and the name(s) and mailing address(es) of persons who are to serve as director(s) until the first annual meeting of shareholders or until their successors are elected and qualify are as follows:

Name and address of director(s)

[fill in name(s)

and address(es)]

SEVENTH: The directors shall have power to make and to alter or amend the bylaws; to fix the amount to be reserved as working capital; and to authorize and cause to be executed mortgages and liens without limit as to the amount upon the property and franchise of the corporation.

With the consent in writing, and pursuant to a vote of the holders of a majority of the capital stock issued and outstanding, the directors shall have the authority to dispose in any manner of the whole property of this corporation.

The bylaws shall determine whether and to what extent the accounts and books of this corporation, or any of them, shall be open to the inspection of the shareholders; and no shareholder shall have any right of inspecting any account or book or document of this corporation, except as conferred by the law or the bylaws, or by resolution of the shareholders.

The shareholders and directors shall have power to hold their meetings and keep the books, documents and papers of the corporation outside of the State of Delaware, at such places as may be from time to time designated by the bylaws or by resolution of the shareholders or directors, except as otherwise required by the laws of Delaware.

It is the intention that the objects, purposes and powers specified in the third paragraph hereof shall, except where otherwise specified in said paragraph, be nowise limited or restricted by reference to or inference from the terms of any other clause or paragraph in this certificate of incorporation, but that the objects, purposes and powers specified in the third paragraph and in each of the clauses or paragraphs of this charter shall be regarded as independent objects, purposes and powers.

EIGHTH: Directors of the corporation shall not be liable to either the corporation or its shareholders for monetary damages for a breach of fiduciary duties unless the breach involves: (1) a director's duty of loyalty to the corporation or its shareholders; (2) acts or omissions not in good faith or which involve intentional misconduct or a knowing violation of law; (3) liability for unlawful payments of dividends or unlawful stock purchases or redemption by the corporation; or (4) a transaction from which the director derived an improper personal benefit.

I, THE UNDERSIGNED, for the purpose of forming a corporation under the laws of the State of Delaware, do make, file and record this certificate and do certify that the facts herein are true; and I have accordingly hereunto set my hand.

DATED AT: _____

State of _____

County of _____
(leave blank unless you are incorporator)

_____
(signature of person or officer of corporation named in fifth article)
(leave blank if using The Company Corporation)

CERTIFICATE OF INCORPORATION
of

_____

FIRST: The name of this corporation is _____

_____

SECOND: Its registered office in the State of Delaware is to be located at _____
_____ in the City of _____ County of _____
_____. The registered agent in charge thereof is _____
_____ at _____.

THIRD: The nature of the business and the objects and purposes to be transacted, promoted and carried on are to do any or all the things herein mentioned as fully and to the same extent as natural persons might or could do, and in any part of the world, viz:

"The purpose of the corporation is to engage in any lawful act or activity for which corporations may be organized under the General Corporation Law of Delaware."

FOURTH: The amount of the total authorized capital stock of this corporation is _____
_____ share of _____ par value.

FIFTH: The name and mailing address of the incorporator is as follows:

NAME: ADDRESS:

_____   _____

                                                     _____

SIXTH: The powers of the incorporator are to terminate upon filing of the certificate of incorporation, and the name(s) and mailing address(es) of persons who are to serve as director(s) until the first annual meeting of shareholders or until their successors are elected and qualify are as follows:

Name and address of director(s)

[fill in name(s)

and address(es)]

SEVENTH: The directors shall have power to make and to alter or amend the bylaws; to fix the amount to be reserved as working capital; and to authorize and cause to be executed mortgages and liens without limit as to the amount upon the property and franchise of the corporation.

With the consent in writing, and pursuant to a vote of the holders of a majority of the capital stock issued and outstanding, the directors shall have the authority to dispose in any manner of the whole property of this corporation.

The bylaws shall determine whether and to what extent the accounts and books of this corporation, or any of them, shall be open to the inspection of the shareholders; and no shareholder shall have any right of inspecting any account or book or document of this corporation, except as conferred by the law or the bylaws, or by resolution of the shareholders.

The shareholders and directors shall have power to hold their meetings and keep the books, documents and papers of the corporation outside of the State of Delaware, at such places as may be from time to time designated by the bylaws or by resolution of the shareholders or directors, except as otherwise required by the laws of Delaware.

It is the intention that the objects, purposes and powers specified in the third paragraph hereof shall, except where otherwise specified in said paragraph, be nowise limited or restricted by reference to or inference from the terms of any other clause or paragraph in this certificate of incorporation, but that the objects, purposes and powers specified in the third paragraph and in each of the clauses or paragraphs of this charter shall be regarded as independent objects, purposes and powers.

EIGHTH: Directors of the corporation shall not be liable to either the corporation or its shareholders for monetary damages for a breach of fiduciary duties unless the breach involves: (1) a director's duty of loyalty to the corporation or its shareholders; (2) acts or omissions not in good faith or which involve intentional misconduct or a knowing violation of law; (3) liability for unlawful payments of dividends or unlawful stock purchases or redemption by the corporation; or (4) a transaction from which the director derived an improper personal benefit.

I, THE UNDERSIGNED, for the purpose of forming a corporation under the laws of the State of Delaware, do make, file and record this certificate and do certify that the facts herein are true; and I have accordingly hereunto set my hand.

DATED AT: _____

State of _____

County of _____
           (leave blank unless you are incorporator)

_____
(signature of person or officer of corporation named in fifth article)
(leave blank if using The Company Corporation)

A CLOSE CORPORATION

SECTION VI

A *close corporation* is a corporation whose certificate of incorporation contains the basic elements contained in a standard Delaware corporation and, in addition, provides the following:

1. All of the corporation's issued stock shall be held by not more than a specified number of persons, not to exceed 30.

2. All of the issued stock shall be subject to one or more restrictions on transfer. The most widely used restriction is one that obligates a shareholder to offer to the corporation or other holders of shares of the corporation a prior opportunity to be exercised within a reasonable time to acquire the restricted securities.

Sometimes other restrictions are included in the Certificate of Incorporation that

A. obligate the corporation to purchase all shares owned by a shareholder pursuant to an agreement regarding the purchase and sale of restricted shares;

B. require the corporation or shareholders of the corporation to consent to any proposed transfer of the restricted shares; or

C. prohibit the transfer of restricted shares to designated persons or classes of persons if such designation is not unreasonable.

Any restriction on the transfer of shares of a corporation for the purpose of maintaining its status as an electing small business corporation under Subchapter S of the Internal Revenue Code is presumed to be for a reasonable purpose.

Another unique feature of a close corporation is that the certificate of incorporation may provide that the business of the corporation shall be managed by the shareholders. No directors need be elected so that no directors meetings are necessary, thus eliminating the formality of directors meetings. Under this feature, the shareholders of the corporation have the powers and responsibilities that directors would normally have.

A close corporation is not permitted to make a public offering of its shares within the meaning of the Securities Act of 1933.

If a shareholder wishes to limit the number of other shareholders and also wants himself or herself and/or other shareholders to have the first opportunity to buy shares from a selling shareholder, a close corporation is the ideal form. This first option to buy shares of stock can be the key to preventing undesirable persons from becoming shareholders in a corporation.

An existing Delaware corporation can elect to be a close corporation if two-thirds of the shareholders vote in favor of it. An amendment to this effect is filed with the Secretary of State in Dover, Delaware.

A close corporation can change its status to a regular or "open" corporation by filing a certificate of amendment with the Secretary of State.

The close corporation was created to allow individuals to operate a corporation in the same informal way they would operate a partnership. Formal meetings are not required and shareholders can act as officers and directors without formal elections. A businessperson who does not expect a business to grow to the extent that it will sell its shares to the public would be well advised to consider forming a close corporation that elects to be an S corporation. This choice means that not only will the corporation benefit from the single-tax status of a partnership but the business can be run in the same informal manner as a partnership.

Another major benefit of close corporation status is that the owners have the right to exclude anyone from becoming a partner and can exercise this option for any reason. A corporation with only two or three owners cannot survive unless those two or three persons can work together. The close corporation option ensures that if one "owner" chooses to sell his or her shares to a stranger, the remaining "owner" can stop that sale by demanding the right to acquire the selling shareholder's shares.

On the following pages is a specimen copy and blank certificates that can be completed should a person wish to form a close corporation. It contains the provisions referred to above.

As with other Delaware corporations, the certificate of incorporation can be filed using any address initially. However, it is preferable to have it filed through a registered agent because a Delaware mailing address is necessary.

CERTIFICATE OF INCORPORATION
of
_____ ABC CORPORATION _____

A CLOSE CORPORATION

FIRST: The name of this corporation is __(repeat proposed name here)__
_____ ABC Corporation _____

SECOND: Its registered office in the State of Delaware is to be located at _Three Christina Centre, 201 North Walnut Street_ in the City of _Wilmington,_ County of _New Castle._ The registered agent in charge thereof is _____ The Company Corporation _____ at address _same as above_ .

THIRD: The nature of the business and the objects and purposes proposed to be transacted, promoted and carried on are to engage in any lawful act or activity for which corporations may be organized under the General Corporation Law of Delaware.

FOURTH: The amount of total authorized capital stock of the corporation is divided into: _# of shares desired i.e., 1500_ shares of _no-par value (unless desire to establish a par value)_ .

FIFTH: The name and mailing address of the incorporator is:

(leave blank if using The Company Corporation as agent, otherwise your name and address)

SIXTH: The powers of the incorporator are to terminate upon filing of the certificate of incorporation, and the name(s) and mailing address(es) of the persons who are to serve as director(s) until the first annual meeting of shareholders or until their successors are elected are as follows:

John Doe, 1 Main Street, Atlantis, CA

SEVENTH: All of the corporation's issued stock, exclusive of treasury shares, shall be held of record by not more than thirty (30) persons.

EIGHTH: All of the issued stock of all classes shall be subject to the following restriction on transfer permitted by Section 202 of the General Corporation Law.

Each shareholder shall offer to the corporation or to other shareholders of the corporation a thirty (30)-day "first refusal" option to purchase the shareholder's stock should the shareholder elect to sell his or her stock.

NINTH: The corporation shall make no offering of any of its stock of any class that would constitute a "public offering" within the meaning of the United States Securities Act of 1933 as it may be amended from time to time.

TENTH: Directors of the corporation shall not be liable to either the corporation or its shareholders for monetary damages for a breach of fiduciary duties unless the breach involves: (1) a director's duty of loyalty to the corporation or its shareholders; (2) acts or omissions not in good faith or which involve intentional misconduct or a knowing violation of law; (3) liability for unlawful payments of dividends or unlawful stock purchases or redemption by the corporation; or (4) a transaction from which the director derived an improper personal benefit.

I, THE UNDERSIGNED, for the purpose of forming a corporation under the laws of the State of Delaware, do make, file and record this certificate, and do certify that the facts herein stated are true; and I have accordingly hereunto set my hand.

DATED AT: _____

John Doe
_____
(signature of person or officer of corporation named in fifth article)
(leave blank if using The Company Corporation)

CERTIFICATE OF INCORPORATION
of

_____

A CLOSE CORPORATION

FIRST: The name of this corporation is _____

_____

SECOND: Its registered office in the State of Delaware is to be located at _____ _____ in the City of _____ County of _____ _____. The registered agent in charge thereof is _____ _____ at _____.

THIRD: The nature of the business and the objects and purposes proposed to be transacted, promoted and carried on are to engage in any lawful act or activity for which corporations may be organized under the General Corporation Law of Delaware.

FOURTH: The amount of total authorized capital stock of the corporation is divided into:

_____ shares of _____

FIFTH: The name and mailing address of the incorporator is:

SIXTH: The powers of the incorporator are to terminate upon filing of the certificate of incorporation, and the name(s) and mailing address(es) of the persons who are to serve as director(s) until the first annual meeting of shareholders or until their successors are elected are as follows:

SEVENTH: All of the corporation's issued stock, exclusive of treasury shares, shall be held of record by not more than thirty (30) persons.

EIGHTH: All of the issued stock of all classes shall be subject to the following restriction on transfer permitted by Section 202 of the General Corporation Law.

Each shareholder shall offer to the corporation or to other shareholders of the corporation a thirty (30)-day "first refusal" option to purchase the shareholder's stock should the shareholder elect to sell his or her stock.

NINTH: The corporation shall make no offering of any of its stock of any class that would constitute a "public offering" within the meaning of the United States Securities Act of 1933, as it may be amended from time to time.

TENTH: Directors of the corporation shall not be liable to either the corporation or its shareholders for monetary damages for a breach of fiduciary duties unless the breach involves: (1) a director's duty of loyalty to the corporation or its shareholders; (2) acts or omissions not in good faith or which involve intentional misconduct or a knowing violation of law; (3) liability for unlawful payments of dividends or unlawful stock purchases or redemption by the corporation; or (4) a transaction from which the director derived an improper personal benefit.

I, THE UNDERSIGNED, for the purpose of forming a corporation under the laws of the State of Delaware, do make, file and record this certificate, and do certify that the facts herein stated are true; and I have accordingly hereunto set my hand.

DATED AT: _____

_____
(signature of person or officer of corporation named in fifth article)
(leave blank if using The Company Corporation)

CERTIFICATE OF INCORPORATION
of

_____

A CLOSE CORPORATION

FIRST: The name of this corporation is _____
_____

SECOND: Its registered office in the State of Delaware is to be located at _____
_____ in the City of _____ County of _____
_____. The registered agent in charge thereof is _____
_____ at _____.

THIRD: The nature of the business and the objects and purposes proposed to be transacted, promoted and carried on are to engage in any lawful act or activity for which corporations may be organized under the General Corporation Law of Delaware.

FOURTH: The amount of total authorized capital stock of the corporation is divided into:
_____ shares of _____

FIFTH: The name and mailing address of the incorporator is:

SIXTH: The powers of the incorporator are to terminate upon filing of the certificate of incorporation, and the name(s) and mailing address(es) of the persons who are to serve as director(s) until the first annual meeting of shareholders or until their successors are elected are as follows:

SEVENTH: All of the corporation's issued stock, exclusive of treasury shares, shall be held of record by not more than thirty (30) persons.

EIGHTH: All of the issued stock of all classes shall be subject to the following restriction on transfer permitted by Section 202 of the General Corporation Law.

Each shareholder shall offer to the corporation or to other shareholders of the corporation a thirty (30)-day "first refusal" option to purchase the shareholder's stock should the shareholder elect to sell his or her stock.

NINTH: The corporation shall make no offering of any of its stock of any class that would constitute a "public offering" within the meaning of the United States Securities Act of 1933, as it may be amended from time to time.

TENTH: Directors of the corporation shall not be liable to either the corporation or its shareholders for monetary damages for a breach of fiduciary duties unless the breach involves: (1) a director's duty of loyalty to the corporation or its shareholders; (2) acts or omissions not in good faith or which involve intentional misconduct or a knowing violation of law; (3) liability for unlawful payments of dividends or unlawful stock purchases or redemption by the corporation; or (4) a transaction from which the director derived an improper personal benefit.

I, THE UNDERSIGNED, for the purpose of forming a corporation under the laws of the State of Delaware, do make, file and record this certificate, and do certify that the facts herein stated are true; and I have accordingly hereunto set my hand.

DATED AT: _____

_____
(signature of person or officer of corporation named in fifth article)
(leave blank if using The Company Corporation)

REGISTERED AGENTS

SECTION VII

In Delaware more than 30 companies provide registered agent services to corporations. Some of these companies are listed later in this section. One of the main functions of these companies is to provide a street address for corporations, because all corporations formed in Delaware are required to have a mailing address in the state. The service companies that can provide this (and other services) are known as registered agents.

Annual fees charged by registered agents for providing a Delaware address range from $75 to $250 per year. One of the largest agents is comprised of several companies and charges $170 per year. If a lawyer's services are used, there are additional fees of $300 to $3000. Registered agents generally charge an additional fee of $60 to $300 for the initial formation of a corporation.

One company, The Company Corporation, charges only $45* per calendar year during the first year for its annual registered agent service. This modest fee is less than that charged by others. This fee increases to $75 for the second year and $99 the third year.

The Company Corporation charges *no initial fee* for the formation of the corporation. No legal fees are necessary since the clients complete the forms themselves. No counseling service is provided or needed if the person who is forming the corporation completes the forms.

Service is provided in a highly confidential and speedy manner. Upon receipt, the corporation forms are filed with the Secretary of State the same day.

Potential savings for using The Company Corporation for the initial formation of the corporation are up to $3,000, and up to $250 on an annual basis.

The Company Corporation operates differently than other registered agents. It operates on a volume basis and advertises for its customers on a direct basis. Its fees are substantially less than its competitors. All middleman fees are eliminated.

The Company Corporation does provide services to customers referred by lawyers, but does not require such referral.

All that is required is that a certificate of incorporation and signed Confidential Information form be completed by the customer and sent to The Company Corporation. The certificate is then forwarded to the appropriate places.

No legal advice or counseling is provided by The Company Corporation. Administerial functions only are provided. No review or advice on the form itself can be given. However, if the form is complete (instructions are contained herein), *none is necessary.* If for any reason the certificate of incorporation is not accepted by the Secretary of State in Dover, Delaware, it is returned without comment by The Company Corporation along with any of the Secretary of State's comments.

In addition to providing a permanent street address in Delaware, The Company Corporation, unlike any other registered agent, provides the following services at no cost to its customers:

Initial Service:

1.   Act as registered agent and provide a mailing address in Delaware. The Company Corporation provides a mailing address for receiving and forwarding all legal documents, not general mail delivery. General mail forwarding can be arranged for an additional fee.

---

* Prices and fees are subject to change without notice.

2. Furnish the incorporator. (Certificate of incorporation can be completed but unsigned if desired.)

3. File the certificate of incorporation with the Corporation Department in Dover, Delaware, via computer.

4. File a copy of the certificate of incorporation with the Recorder of Deeds' office.

5. Prepare checks for payment of initial recording fees to the State of Delaware.

6. Reserve corporate name and file documents the same day request is received from customer.

7. Prepare printed stock certificates, corporate seal and forms for minutes and bylaws if the client desires the option.

8. Supply the appropriate forms for qualifying the Delaware corporation in any other state in the United States at the nominal handling charge—$.50 each—upon request.

Continuing Services:

9. Process application for federal identification number.

10. Process application for S-status filings with the IRS.

11. Process qualifications in other states and act as registered agent in qualified states.

12. Act as registered agent and provide a mailing address in Delaware.

13. Forward the corporation's annual report form from the Secretary of State, Dover, Delaware. Once each year the Delaware Secretary of State sends an annual report form to the Delaware mailing address of every corporation chartered in the state. The Company Corporation forwards this to its customers. It is completed by the customer and sent back to the Secretary of State, Dover, Delaware, for filing. If you prefer, The Company Corporation can process and handle all paperwork for you at a modest fee.

14. Assist in locating facilities for annual meetings if the client wishes to have them and/or hold them in Delaware.

15. Receive legal documents served on the corporation in Delaware, including lawsuits, and forward these to the business address of the corporation.

16. Publish a periodic newsletter dealing with helpful business ideas that can save money. Other products and services that The Company Corporation makes available to its customers are described in the newsletter, including helpful books and manuals, and patent and trademark searches.

In addition, The Company Corporation will furnish upon request the Delaware fee schedule for filing forms with the state. These include, but are not limited to, forms for increases in the number of shares of stock, new classes of stock, amending certificates of incorporation, dissolutions and the like.

A partial list of companies in Delaware that are available to provide services to corporations, including acting as registered agent, are listed as follows:

No initial fee for filing corporate documents	THE COMPANY CORPORATION
No legal fees necessary	THREE CHRISTNA CENTRE
Annual Fee: $45 first calendar year	201 NORTH WALNUT STREET
$75 second calendar year	WILMINGTON, DE 19801
$99 third year and thereafter	

Initial Fee $60–$300 for filing corporate documents. Legal Fees $300–$3,000 (most of these companies require that clients be referred by a lawyer). Annual Fee $75–$250.

American Guaranty & Trust Co.
3801 Kennett Pike
Greenville Center
Wilmington, Delaware 19807

Capital Trust Co. of Delaware
1013 Centre Rd.
Wilmington, Delaware 19805

Corporate Systems Inc.
101 North Fairfield Dr.
Dover, Delaware 19801

Corporation Guarantee & Trust Co.
11th Fl., Rodney Square North
11th & Market Streets
Wilmington, Delaware 19801

Corporation Trust Co. (The)
1209 Orange Street
Wilmington, Delaware 19801

Delaware Corporation Organizers, Inc.
1105 North Market Street
Wilmington, Delaware 19899

Delaware Registration Trust Co.
900 Market Street
Wilmington, Delaware 19801

Delaware Registry, Ltd.
2316 Baynard Blvd.
Wilmington, Delaware 19802

Incorporating Services, Ltd.
410 South State Street
Dover, Delaware 19901

Incorporators of Delaware
48 The Green
Dover, Delaware 19901

National Corporate Research, Ltd.
15 North Street
Dover, Delaware 19901

Prentice-Hall Corp. System, Inc. (The)
229 South State Street
Dover, Delaware 19901

Registered Agents, Ltd.
902 Market Street
Wilmington, Delaware 19899

United Corporate Services, Inc.
229 South State Street
Dover, Delaware 19901

United States Corporation Co.
229 South State Street
Dover, Delaware 19901

THE COMPANY CORPORATION

SECTION VIII

Any registered agent listed in this book can assist in filing forms for incorporating and providing other services to corporations. The Company Corporation provides its services in a different manner and at a lower cost than any other company; also, it will assist you in incorporating in the State of Delaware or in any other state. If you want to incorporate in a state other than Delaware, call 1-800-542-2677 and ask for a complete set of forms and information for the state that interests you. Details will be furnished to all buyers of this book free of charge.

The Company Corporation charges no fee for initial administerial services in filing the certificate of incorporation with the State of Delaware, providing that The Company Corporation is appointed registered agent. Other registered agents charge up to $300 for initial incorporating services in addition to a lawyer's fee. The annual fee for engaging The Company Corporation is $45 during the first year with no legal fees. The fee gradually increases to $75 the second year and $99 the third year and thereafter. This modest graduating fee is designed to help keep costs as low as possible during the corporation's early formative years.

The only other initial costs to the incorporator are Delaware fees plus the registered agent fee as follows:

$ 25	covers the cost of filing, receiving and indexing the certificate;
15	is the minimum state tax (authorized capitalization not exceeding $75,000 or 1,500 no-par shares; 1,500 shares, as previously suggested, result in the lowest fees);
10	for a certified copy from the state;
24	for a *one-page* certificate; and
45	first calendar-year fee for registered agent service
$119	aggregate amount paid to The Company Corporation at the time the charter is filed.

Most certificates of incorporation run unnecessarily to four or more pages costing $42 or more just to file. The forms in this book, most on one page except nonstock forms, cost only $9 per page plus a $6 document recording fee ($24 minimum) to file with the Recorder of Deeds. Copy used in the certificates of incorporation contained in this book has been reproduced from forms supplied by the Secretary of State, Dover, Delaware.

Minutes of the first meeting and bylaws may be torn out of this book and used for the new corporation. Stock certificates and corporate seals are available from stationery stores.

As an option to its customers, The Company Corporation makes available a corporate kit that contains the following:

1. A vinyl-covered record book to hold corporate records (with extra-large holes) size 12″ × 10″ × 1.5″ with the corporate name printed on a gold insert.

2. A metal corporate seal (in a pouch) imprinted with the corporate name 1⅝″ in diameter. This can be used on various documents.

3. Twenty lithographed stock certificates of one class of stock printed with the corporate name and capitalization. (If there is more than one class of stock, you may request the price.)

4. Preprinted minute and bylaw forms to fit into the record book (also available on diskette).

5. A stock/transfer ledger for keeping an accurate and complete record of your corporate stock, including stock transfers.

6. Standard forms for your Delaware Corporation's management (a $54.95 value). See p. 39 for details.

The total minimum cost for utilizing The Company Corporation as a registered agent in the State of Delaware is $119. With the above optional and useful material, the additional cost is $79.95, plus $8.00 for U.P.S. delivery, making a total of $206.95. Details and costs for incorporating in other states are available upon request.

By popular request, The Company Corporation will apply for and obtain a federal tax I.D. number and S status for each corporation for the nominal fee of $70. Allow 60 days for normal IRS turnaround time, which is usually faster than if done by a client individually. Also, if you need a federal tax I.D. number sooner, The Company Corporation has an expedited service that can obtain your number in just five to seven business days for an additional $40 (not available in all locations).

Delaware & County Fee	Incorporating Fee—Using The Company Corporation First Year's* Registered Agent Fee	Total
$74.00	$45.00	$119.00
	Optional Corporate Kit ($79.95 + $8.00 UPS)	87.95
	Apply for S Corporation Status (optional)	35.00
	Federal I.D. Number (optional)	35.00
Total Payable to The Company Corporation—including Kit		$276.95**

In rare cases there may be a need for a corporation that differs slightly from the examples in this book, involving more than one class of stock, more shares or the like. The Company Corporation will furnish quotations of what the State of Delaware's filing fees are for any type of corporation. In no case does The Company Corporation charge more than the $45 annual registered agent fee for filing initial documents so long as they are completed by the customer.

The Company Corporation cannot furnish personal counsel or advice or answer questions to inquiries that involve interpretations or opinions of law.

Annual registered agent fee is payable each calendar year. Calendar year begins on January 1.

** *All prices and fees subject to change without notice.*

CONFIDENTIAL INFORMATION FORM

To incorporate now call toll-free: 1-800-542-2677 or fax to: 1-302-575-1346

1. Name of Corporation: Name must have corporate ending such as Inc., Corporation, etc. (Inc. will be used if nothing is provided.)

_____

Alternate name(s): (If above is reserved or already in use by another corporation)

_____

_____

2. Nature of business the company will transact:

_____

_____

3. State of Incorporation: _____

4. Type of business structure: Check one.

☐ Open

☐ Close

☐ Non-stock/Non-profit

☐ LLC

☐ Other_____

5. Number of shares of common stock: _____

(Up to 1,500 at lowest cost in Delaware)

These shares shall be 1500@ no par value unless otherwise specified.

Or _____ at $_____ par value.

6. Principal office outside state of incorporation:

_____

_____

7. Number of Directors: _____

8. Name(s) and addresses of Director(s):

Delaware requires just one, who may also be an officer. Directors' names will not appear on Delaware Certificates of Incorporation.

_____

_____

_____

_____

_____

_____

_____

_____

_____

9. Names of officer(s):

(One person may hold all offices in Delaware.)

President _____

Secretary _____

Vice President _____

Treasurer _____

10. Please send all correspondence relevant to this corporation to:

Name _____

Address _____

_____

City _____

State: _____ Zip: _____

Daytime Telephone (____) _____ – _____

Fax Number (____) _____ – _____

11. Special instructions, if required:

_____

_____

_____

I certify that neither The Company Corporation nor any of its employees or agents have provided me with any personal counsel or advice. *(We cannot proceed with your incorporation without your signature.)*

✐ Signature _____

Date _____

12. How did you learn of our services?

☐ Advertisement in _____

(Please include extension or Dept. # in advertisement)

☐ Book

☐ Direct Mail

☐ Referred by _____

(Please let us know, we'd like to say thanks)

☐ Other

CONFIDENTIAL INFORMATION FORM

To incorporate now call toll-free: 1-800-542-2677 or fax to: 1-302-575-1346

▶ **Name of Corporation:** _____

▶ **State Filing Fees:**
Delaware for profit, $74.00
Delaware non-stock non-profit, $83.00
Please call for fees in other states.

$ [   ]

▶ **Registered Agent Fees:** First calendar year service $45 for Delaware, $100 all other states.

$ [   ]

▶ **Corporate Kit** (Check one.)

Delaware Deluxe:	$177.95
Delaware Standard:	$ 87.95

Both of the above kits include "Standard Forms for Your Delaware Corporation's Management" — a $49.95 value

Non-Delaware Deluxe:	$177.95
Non-Delaware Standard:	$ 87.95
LLCs — For all states:	$ 97.95

$ [   ]

All prices include shipping & handling. Canada and Puerto Rico please add $15.

▶ **Standard Forms for Your Delaware Corporation's Management:** $49.95 + $5.00 S&H = $54.95 $ [   ]

▶ **Minutes and By-Laws Forms on Diskette:** $39.95 + $5.00 S&H = $44.95 $ [   ]

▶ **Tax-On-Time:** (Delaware corporations only) $30.00 or $80.00 $ [   ]
After Sept. 1, please include additional $50.00 for minimum State Franchise Tax and filing fee.

▶ **Federal Tax I.D. Number:** (Application in your confirmation package) $35.00 $ [   ]
Expedited Service: i.e., 7 - 10 business days from our receipt of your
completed application (not available for all locations) $75.00

▶ **Apply for "S" Corporation Status:** (Application in your confirmation package) $35.00 $ [   ]
(IRS processing time: 4 - 6 weeks from our receipt of your completed application)

▶ **Premium Mail Forwarding Service:** (Delaware corporations only) $225.00 for 6 months $ [   ]

▶ **Basic Mail Forwarding Service:** (Delaware corporations only) $42.00 per year $ [   ]

▶ **Complete Book of Corporate Forms:**

☐ Book $69.95 + $8.00 S&H = $77.95
☐ Diskette; please specify: ☐ IBM ☐ MAC $69.95 + $5.00 S&H = $74.95
☐ Book and Diskette Special Package **(Save $20)** $119.95 + $8.00 S&H = $127.95

▶ **Delaware Shelf Corporation:** Call for exact fee. $ [   ]

▶ **Trademark Search:** *Quoted prices are minimum.* $ [   ]
☐ Basic search $175.00
☐ Patent and Trademark Office Search $195.00
☐ Comprehensive Trademark Search $350.00

▶ **Processing Fees**: If we are not your Registered Agent $200.00 $ [   ]

TOTAL: $ [   ]

───

☐ Enclosed is a check drawn on a U.S. bank payable to The Company Corporation in the amount of $_____
NOTE: *For rapid service, enclose a certified check, treasurer's check, money order, or credit card information.
Otherwise please allow fourteen (14) days for check clearance.*

PAYMENT INFORMATION

☐ Charge my: ☐ Visa ☐ MasterCard

Card Number: _____ Exp. Date: _____

✎ Signature _____

CONFIDENTIAL INFORMATION FORM
To incorporate now call toll-free: 1-800-542-2677 or fax to: 1-302-575-1346

1. Name of Corporation: Name must have corporate ending such as Inc., Corporation, etc. (Inc. will be used if nothing is provided.)

_____

Alternate name(s): (If above is reserved or already in use by another corporation)

_____

2. Nature of business the company will transact:

_____

3. State of Incorporation: _____

4. Type of business structure: Check one.
- ☐ Open
- ☐ Close
- ☐ Non-stock/Non-profit
- ☐ LLC
- ☐ Other_____

5. Number of shares of common stock: _____
(Up to 1,500 at lowest cost in Delaware)
These shares shall be 1500@ no par value unless otherwise specified.

Or _____ at $_____ par value.

6. Principal office outside state of incorporation:

_____

_____

7. Number of Directors: _____

8. Name(s) and addresses of Director(s):
Delaware requires just one, who may also be an officer. Directors' names will not appear on Delaware Certificates of Incorporation.

_____

_____

_____

_____

_____

_____

_____

9. Names of officer(s):
(One person may hold all offices in Delaware.)

President _____

Secretary _____

Vice President _____

Treasurer _____

10. Please send all correspondence relevant to this corporation to:

Name _____

Address _____

_____

City _____

State: _____ Zip: _____

Daytime Telephone ( ) – _____

Fax Number ( ) – _____

11. Special instructions, if required:

_____

_____

I certify that neither The Company Corporation nor any of its employees or agents have provided me with any personal counsel or advice. _(We cannot proceed with your incorporation without your signature.)_

✍ Signature _____

Date _____

12. How did you learn of our services?
- ☐ Advertisement in _____
  (Please include extension or Dept. # in advertisement)
- ☐ Book
- ☐ Direct Mail
- ☐ Referred by _____
  (Please let us know, we'd like to say thanks)
- ☐ Other _____

CONFIDENTIAL INFORMATION FORM

To incorporate now call toll-free: 1-800-542-2677 or fax to: 1-302-575-1346

▶ **Name of Corporation:** _____

▶ **State Filing Fees:** $ [   ]
   Delaware for profit, $74.00
   Delaware non-stock non-profit, $83.00
   Please call for fees in other states.

▶ **Registered Agent Fees:** First calendar year service $45 for Delaware, $100 all other states. $ [   ]

▶ **Corporate Kit** (Check one.) $ [   ]
   Delaware Deluxe: $177.95
   Delaware Standard: $ 87.95
   Both of the above kits include "Standard Forms for Your Delaware Corporation's Management" — a $49.95 value
   Non-Delaware Deluxe: $177.95
   Non-Delaware Standard: $ 87.95
   LLCs — For all states: $ 97.95
   All prices include shipping & handling. Canada and Puerto Rico please add $15.

▶ **Standard Forms for Your Delaware Corporation's Management:** $49.95 + $5.00 S&H = $54.95 $ [   ]

▶ **Minutes and By-Laws Forms on Diskette:** $39.95 + $5.00 S&H = $44.95 $ [   ]

▶ **Tax-On-Time:** (Delaware corporations only) $30.00 or $80.00 $ [   ]
   After Sept. 1, please include additional $50.00 for minimum State Franchise Tax and filing fee.

▶ **Federal Tax I.D. Number:** (Application in your confirmation package) $35.00 $ [   ]
   Expedited Service: i.e., 7 - 10 business days from our receipt of your
   completed application (not available for all locations) $75.00

▶ **Apply for "S" Corporation Status:** (Application in your confirmation package) $35.00 $ [   ]
   (IRS processing time: 4 - 6 weeks from our receipt of your completed application)

▶ **Premium Mail Forwarding Service:** (Delaware corporations only) $225.00 for 6 months $ [   ]

▶ **Basic Mail Forwarding Service:** (Delaware corporations only) $42.00 per year $ [   ]

▶ **Complete Book of Corporate Forms:**

   ☐ Book $69.95 + $8.00 S&H = $77.95
   ☐ Diskette; please specify: ☐ IBM ☐ MAC $69.95 + $5.00 S&H = $74.95
   ☐ Book and Diskette Special Package **(Save $20)** $119.95 + $8.00 S&H = $127.95

▶ **Delaware Shelf Corporation:** Call for exact fee. $ [   ]

▶ **Trademark Search:** *Quoted prices are minimum.* $ [   ]
   ☐ Basic search $175.00
   ☐ Patent and Trademark Office Search $195.00
   ☐ Comprehensive Trademark Search $350.00

▶ **Processing Fees**: If we are not your Registered Agent $200.00 $ [   ]
TOTAL: $ [   ]

....

☐ Enclosed is a check drawn on a U.S. bank payable to The Company Corporation in the amount of $_____
   NOTE: *For rapid service, enclose a certified check, treasurer's check, money order, or credit card information.*
   Otherwise please allow fourteen (14) days for check clearance.

PAYMENT INFORMATION

☐ Charge my: ☐ Visa   ☐ MasterCard

   Card Number: _____   Exp. Date: _____

   ✍ Signature _____

PROTECT YOUR CORPORATION'S VALUABLE LEGAL STATUS *with an* EASY-TO-USE CORPORATE KIT

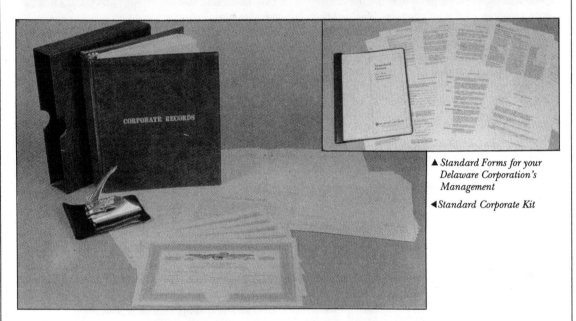

▲ *Standard Forms for your Delaware Corporation's Management*

◀ *Standard Corporate Kit*

THE COMPLETE PERSONALIZED KIT INCLUDES:

1. Your personalized Corporate Binder with slipcase — protects your corporate records. Your corporate name will be printed on a gold inset on the spine of this handsome binder.

2. Your personalized corporate seal can be kept in a pouch inside your binder. Use your corporate seal for completion of legal documents such as leases and purchase agreements.

Your corporate name and year of incorporation will be permanently etched into the dies which create a raised impression on any paper. *(Separately, seal is $25 for up to 45 characters.)*

3. For your permanent records: minutes & by-laws forms printed on three-hole paper for easy record-keeping. Complete forms included for any corporation. *(Also available on diskette)*

4. 20 personalized stock certificates lithographed with your corporate name on each certificate. Printing also includes number of shares authorized by corporation. *(Additional stock certificates can be purchased. Minimum purchase is 20 @ $25.50 total, 21 to 99 @ .85 each; over 100 @ .50 each)*

5. Celluloid tab index separators make it easy to turn to any section in your binder.

6. Stock/transfer ledger — to keep an accurate and complete record of your corporate stock, including stock transfers.

In kits for Delaware corporations only, you will also receive **FREE** *Standard Forms for Your Delaware Corporation's Management, the most commonly used forms for corporate maintenance, complete with instructions and fee schedules.*

YOUR CHOICE *of* LUXURIOUS CORPORATE KITS

DELUXE CORPORATE KIT
$177.95 *(All States)*

Crafted with the finest attention to detail, this deluxe edition corporate binder with matching slipcase will become a classic addition to your office, boardroom or library. With your corporate name embossed on the binder in gold, this elegant all-in-one kit comes complete with the items listed on page 8 (and for Delaware Corporations, with Standard Forms for Your Delaware Corporation's Management).

STANDARD DELAWARE CORPORATE KIT
$87.95

The handsome binder and matching slipcase are quality constructed with a burgundy finish. Comes complete with the necessities listed on the facing page, plus Standard Forms for Your Delaware Corporation's Management. Your corporate name is imprinted on a gold inset on the spine. Makes record-keeping efficient and easy.

STANDARD NON-DELAWARE CORPORATE KIT
$87.95 *(Same style as standard Delaware Corporate Kit, but does not include Standard Forms.)*

STANDARD KIT FOR LLCS
$97.95

This handsomely designed kit includes limited liability membership certificates, a seal with pouch, a special agreement section and a forms section. The turned-edged 3-ring binder and matching slipcase will be personalized with the name of your LLC on its spine.

STANDARD FORMS FOR YOUR DELAWARE CORPORATION'S MANAGEMENT
$54.95 *(If purchased separately)*

The most commonly used forms for corporate maintenance, complete with instructions and fee schedules.

MINUTES AND BY-LAWS ON DISKETTE
$44.95

Maintenance of your corporate records is now easier... all minutes and by-laws in your corporate kit are now available on diskette and can be personalized using your own computer. IBM Diskettes are available in 3-1/2".

WE STRIVE FOR TOTAL CUSTOMER SATISFACTION!

If for any reason you are not totally satisfied with your kit, call us, and we'll exchange the product or give you a full refund.

The Company Corporation cannot furnish personal counsel or advice or answer questions or inquiries that involve interpretations or opinions of law.

THE COMPANY CORPORATION

PROVIDING CORPORATE SERVICES *to* BUSINESSES SINCE 1972.

© *1996 The Company Corporation*

EXISTING CORPORATIONS THAT WISH TO
CHANGE REGISTERED AGENTS

SECTION IX

In order for an existing *Delaware* corporation to obtain the advantages offered by The Company Corporation, only a simple form is necessary. If a person wishes to change agents, the total cost to that corporation the first year is $99. This is the actual filing cost that is paid to the State of Delaware and is less than existing corporations are charged by their present registered agents each year. The fee is $75 to file the form with the Secretary of State and $24 to the Recorder of Deeds for a total of $99.

The Company Corporation will provide its registered agent services at no cost during the first calendar year to existing corporations. Thereafter, its annual fee is $99. This is an annual savings of at least $25 and up to $200.

A specimen of the Delaware form that makes it possible to change registered agents is on the next page.

If you wish to avail yourself of this low-cost service, write The Company Corporation for a copy of this form in duplicate. By mailing this form and a completed confidential information form with a check for $99 (payable to The Company Corporation), the certification document will be forwarded to the Secretary of State's office in Dover, Delaware, for filing.

If the corporation has its present office in Kent or Sussex County, prepare an additional copy of the form and add $8 to the amount, making a total of $105.

(To Be Submitted in Duplicate)

CERTIFICATE OF CHANGE OF LOCATION OF REGISTERED
OFFICE AND REGISTERED AGENT
OF

_____

The board of directors of the _____,
a corporation of Delaware, on this _____ day of _____ A.D. 19____ do hereby resolve and order that the location of the registered office of this corporation within this State be, and the same hereby is _____, in the City of _____
_____, in the County of _____.

The name of the registered agent therein and in charge thereof upon whom process against this corporation may be served is _____.

The _____, a corporation of Delaware, doth hereby certify that the foregoing is a true copy of a resolution adopted by the board of directors at a meeting held as herein stated.

IN WITNESS WHEREOF, said corporation has caused this certificate to be signed by its President and attested by its Secretary, and its corporate seal to be hereto affixed, the _____ day of _____
____ A.D. 19____.

By _____

(SEAL)   President

ATTEST:

_____
Secretary

STATE FEE FOR QUALIFYING DELAWARE CORPORATIONS IN OTHER STATES

SECTION X

A Delaware corporation that has all or most of its activities in another state is supposed to register—qualify—the corporation in that other state. Many Delaware corporations fail to register or qualify in other states, but a hazard in not doing so is usually a small fine and payment of a registration fee. Also, the unqualified Delaware corporation may not be able to use the courts of another state. Anyone can write to the Secretary of State in any state to determine its policy on "foreign" corporations that have not registered within that state.

On the following pages are the fees and taxes charged by each state for qualifying a Delaware corporation in another state as a foreign corporation (e.g., if a Minnesota resident has a business in Minnesota and forms a Delaware corporation, that resident is supposed to pay the home state a fee for qualifying a foreign corporation). The qualification procedure for foreign corporations is simple and can be accomplished at any time. A Delaware registered agent can file a copy of the certificate of incorporation with any particular state or states anytime during the life of the corporation. The Company Corporation provides this service to its customers at a processing cost of $50.

There are businesses that legally circumvent paying fees to their home state by establishing that they are "doing business" in Delaware and not in another state. Examples would include corporations that receive and ship materials from Delaware, mail order businesses that use a Delaware office, corporations that own property in Delaware, and franchise or licensing companies that transact all contracts and orders in Delaware.

As to out-of-state residents who incorporate in Delaware, the Secretary of State's office in Dover, Delaware, does not notify any other state who the new Delaware corporation owners or shareholders are or in what state they have a business office.

The following chart lists the fees for qualifying a Delaware corporation in another state. The fees charged by the various states are, of course, subject to change. If an additional certified copy of a Delaware certificate of incorporation is required by another state, Delaware's fee is $21 for a one-page certificate. A certificate of good standing, required by some states, is $20.

QUALIFICATION OF A DELAWARE CORPORATION
(One-Time Fee)

SECTION X-A

Each state's Corporation Department assesses fees to all corporations foreign to that state:

	For-Profit Corp.	Not-for-Profit Corp.
Alabama	$225	$75
Alaska	365	65
Arizona	175	175
Arkansas	300	300
California	1,150	55
Colorado	75	75
Connecticut	275	20
District of Columbia	152	12
Florida	70	70
Georgia	170	70
Hawaii	150*	25
Idaho	100	30
Illinois	100*	50
Indiana	90	30
Iowa	100	25
Kansas	95	95
Kentucky	90	40
Louisiana	100	100
Maine	180	25
Maryland	50	50
Massachusetts	300	300
Michigan	60	20
Minnesota	200	50
Mississippi	525	125
Missouri	155	15
Montana	120	20
Nebraska	145	25
Nevada	135	35
New Hampshire	85	25
New Jersey	100	100
New Mexico	200	25
New York	225	135
N. Carolina	200	100
N. Dakota	135	50

	For-Profit Corp.	Not-for-Profit Corp.
Ohio	$100	$ 35
Oklahoma	300	300
Oregon	440	40
Pennsylvania	180	180
Rhode Island	165*	50
S. Carolina	135	10
S. Dakota	40*	50
Tennessee	600	600
Texas	750	25
Utah	75	30
Vermont	100	50
Virginia	75*	75
Washington	175	30
W. Virginia	192–320**	20
Wisconsin	100*	no fee
Wyoming	80	10

---

 * These states require a certified copy of the corporation's certificate of incorporation and/or a certificate of good standing.

** West Virginia uses a sliding-scale fee range based on the month an application is made. January is the most expensive month ($320) and December the least expensive ($195). A monthly breakdown is available from the West Virginia Department of Corporations; call 304-558-6000.

TOTAL APPROXIMATE QUALIFICATION
FEES FOR ALL 50 STATES: $10,232

SECTION X-B

Either certified copies of certificates of incorporation (also called articles of incorporation) or certificates of good standing are required in most states. Additional copies of a validated certificate of incorporation can be obtained from the Secretary of State's office in Dover, Delaware. The cost is $21 for a certified copy of the certificate of incorporation and $20 for a certificate of good standing.

(The Company Corporation will supply you with qualification forms for any state at $0.50 each for postage and handling.)

As legislation can and does change rapidly, it is advisable to check with the individual state regarding current fee schedules and regulations.

MINIMUM INCORPORATION FEE PAYABLE TO
CORPORATION DEPARTMENT
FOR DOMESTIC CORPORATIONS

SECTION XI

	For-Profit Corp.	Not-for-Profit Corp.
Alabama	$85	$45
Alaska	250	50
Arizona	60	40
Arkansas	50	50
California	900	55
Colorado	50	50
Connecticut	275	65
Delaware	70	70
District of Columbia	120	12
Florida	70	70
Georgia	100	100
Hawaii	50	25
Idaho	100	30
Illinois	100	50
Indiana	90	30
Iowa	50	20
Kansas	75	20
Kentucky	50	8
Louisiana	60	60
Maine	105	20
Maryland	40	40
Massachusetts	200	35
Michigan	60	20
Minnesota	135	70
Mississippi	50	50
Missouri	58	15
Montana	70	20
Nebraska	65	10
Nevada	135	35
New Hampshire	85	25
New Jersey	100	50
New Mexico	100	25
New York	155	75
N. Carolina	100	40

	For-Profit Corp.	Not-for-Profit Corp.
N. Dakota	$ 90	$ 40
Ohio	85	25
Oklahoma	50	25
Oregon	50	20
Pennsylvania	100	100
Rhode Island	150	35
S. Carolina	235	25
S. Dakota	40	20
Tennessee	100	100
Texas	300	25
Utah	75	30
Vermont	75	35
Virginia	75	75
Washington	175	30
W. Virginia	192–320*	20
Wisconsin	90	35
Wyoming	90	10

---

* West Virginia uses a sliding-scale fee range based on the month an application is made. January is the most expensive month ($320) and December the least expensive ($195). A monthly breakdown is available from the West Virginia Department of Corporations; call 304-558-6000.

COMMON, PREFERRED, VOTING AND NONVOTING STOCK

SECTION XII

A corporation may issue common or preferred stock with or without par value.

Usually preferred shareholders have priority rights over common shareholders with respect to dividends and in the event a corporation is liquidated or dissolved. Also, preferred stock usually does not include voting privileges.

Stock in a corporation may also have conditions imposed upon it that permit shareholders either to have or not to have voting privileges. Voting or nonvoting stock is usually designated by class, such as class A voting stock and class B nonvoting stock.

Capital stock can also be issued with a stated value paid for in cash or by providing services to the corporation. However, under Delaware's corporate law, no capital is required by a Delaware corporation.

A Delaware corporation may file simple forms with the Secretary of State to add provisions for any of the above types of stock at any time after the corporation is formed.

The forms in this book are directed to a corporation with one class of stock. No-par common stock shares (with voting privileges) of up to 1,500 shares are used in the specimen forms. The filing fees, both initial and continuing, are lowest with this type of format. Also, this kind of approach to the type of stock is simple and services the needs of most small and medium-sized corporations.

On an annual basis, a franchise tax is based on the number of authorized shares of stock, irrespective of par value. It's an unnecessary expense to authorize more shares of stock than that necessary to meet the needs of the corporation. On 1,500 shares the annual tax is only $30. Examples of fees for more shares are as follows: on 100,000 shares it is $385 and on 1,000,000 shares it is $3,535.

If, however, it is desirable to issue other classes of stock initially, this can be easily accomplished by adding language to this effect on the certificate of incorporation before it is filed with the state.

The state filing fees for the various types of stock may be obtained from the Secretary of State, Dover, Delaware, or a registered agent.

NO-PAR VERSUS PAR VALUE STOCK

SECTION XIII

Prior to the 1940s, it was customary for most corporations to issue *par value* stock. This meant that each share had a stated value on its face, such as $3, which supposedly represented the amount contributed by the shareholder. However, the value of a share of stock can fluctuate greatly, depending on the overall worth of the corporation, so the par value of the stock becomes misleading and unimportant.

Another type of stock has therefore become increasingly more popular. It is called *no-par value* stock. In all respects but one, *no-par value* and *par value* stock are identical. Under the *no-par* method, a certificate of stock has no stated value but merely indicates the number of shares of *no-par value*. The actual value would depend on what an investor is willing to pay, and this judgment is based on a number of factors. These factors include the assets owned by the corporation and the assessment by investors of the corporation's potential profitability.

In addition, the initial filing fee and annual fees to the State of Delaware are lowest when the corporation issues 1,500 shares or less than $75,000 contributed capital. The minimum filing fee is only $15. The type of stock used as examples in this book is no-par. A corporation can convert its no-par value stock to par value stock merely by filing a simple form with the State of Delaware. This form can be forwarded to the Secretary of State by a registered agent, including The Company Corporation, for a nominal filing fee. On the whole, it's usually simpler and less costly to form a Delaware corporation and qualify it to do business in any state with its shares being no-par.

If a corporation becomes successful and authorizes more shares, as well as acquires substantial assets, there can be substantial annual savings in Delaware corporate franchise taxes from converting the no-par value stock to par value stock.

To raise capital, a corporation can also issue bonds that are usually an interest-bearing instrument. A *bond* is a form of debt financing many corporations prefer over the sale of stock.

In business judgments involving decisions of this type, many times it is desirable to consider ideas of authors, accountants, life insurance advisers, trust officers, lawyers and other sources of information.

ONLY ONE OFFICER NEEDED

SECTION XIV

The Delaware corporation needs only one person to hold all the company offices. This same individual may also act as the incorporator and be the entire board of directors. One officer is the legal minimum.

On the other hand, one can have as many directors, officers or vice presidents as desired. Many corporations find it helpful to invite to their boards of directors capable people who may make substantial contributions to building a successful corporation.

A new amendment to Delaware's corporate law provides substantially greater flexibility than ever before in many areas, including a reduction in the number of officers from a minimum of three to one. Previously, a corporation had to have at least three officers—president, secretary and treasurer. The only requirement now is one officer, which enables the corporation to have a person available to sign stock certificates and keep minutes of shareholder and directors' meetings when appropriate.

THE CORPORATE NAME

SECTION XV

The name picked for the new corporation when it is submitted to Delaware will be recorded as long as it is in proper form and no one else is using the same name or one that is too similar prior to the application of the new corporation. *The name must contain the word association, corporation, club, foundation, fund, company, incorporated, institute, society, union, syndicate, limited or one of the abbreviations—Co., Corp. Inc. or Ltd.*

Delaware will permit words like the ones above in abbreviated form, provided they are written in Roman characters or letters. Corporate names must be distinguishable on the records of the state from the names of other corporations formed under the laws of Delaware.

The state provides a service whereby a corporate name can be reserved for a period of 30 days at a charge of $10. Any person can write or call the state directly to avail himself or herself of this service. The Company Corporation provides this service at no charge if appointed registered agent for the corporation. Registered agents provide this service, usually at low cost.

Certain property rights under the law accrue to the original owners of a business name or to a corporation that originates a name. These businesses may legally prevent a new firm from using a name that is the same or similar to theirs. If it is planned that the corporation will qualify as a foreign corporation (see Section X) in any state, the corporate name is registered in that state by the act of such a filing. Sometimes a name is available in Delaware but not in another state in which the corporation wishes to qualify. When this occurs, the corporate name can easily be changed. The filing cost is $100 and another $24 to the Recorder of Deeds for a total of $124. The form is available from the Secretary of State, Dover, Delaware. Your registered agent can also assist you at a modest cost.

POTENTIAL PROBLEMS WITH A CORPORATION'S NAME

The effect of a name change varies. Sometimes it just involves new stationery and notification to people with whom the corporation does business. In other cases a substantial cost can be incurred (e.g., when a large inventory of packaged goods bears the name). Some businesses use a name change to marketing advantage. Many well established corporations choose to change their name to create a different image or to reflect a different line of products or services than they had when the corporation was formed. It is wise to check the yellow pages of the telephone directory when first planning to use a name to see if similar ones exist.

To reduce the need for a name change, one can contact the Corporation Department in any state to determine if the name is available before filing the form.

When you know that an existing business uses a certain name, it is prudent not to select a name that is similar regardless of where that business is located. Theoretically, a name can be registered in all 50 states to avoid the possibility of a later name change. However, owners of corporations seldom go to this extent. Also, an unincorporated business somewhere in the United States may be using the same name that the corporation might use, and the right to the name could be challenged at some future time. Therefore, unless one were to search every business name in the nation on a regular basis, there is always the possibility of a need for a name change at some time during the life of a corporation.

OPERATING ANONYMOUSLY IF DESIRED

SECTION XVI

Many people who own Delaware corporations prefer to remain as anonymous as possible.

In Delaware, a corporation need not disclose who its shareholders are to the Secretary of State. If a person does not wish to disclose who the officer(s) and/or director(s) is, there are three ways to accomplish this.

1. *The first method is by having an acquaintance, friend or relative of the founder(s) hold all the company offices.* This person does not have to be a shareholder in the corporation. (This person, however, should be advised that he or she could be liable in the event of·a tax delinquency or for any illegal action by the founder.)

2. *The second way is to obtain and register a legal fictitious name.* (Many authors use this approach, commonly called a pen name.) A fictitious name can be registered in a prothonotary's office in Delaware for $15. Other states have a similar procedure. Then this name can be used for corporate purposes, such as to sign checks and the like. A fictitious name may be registered where you reside with the Recorder of Deeds or a prothonotary's office (or its equivalent, such as a county clerk's office) or in Delaware.

3. *The third method is by the corporation's not filing its annual report with the Secretary of State.* This report is a simple form that is completed once each year. It basically indicates who the corporation's officers are, how many shares of stock have been authorized and other data on the corporation's assets. It lists officer(s), director(s) and number of shares. The state imposes a $50 annual fine on corporations that do not file this report. Many Delaware corporations have elected in the past to pay this annual fine rather than file the report, although the state frowns on this practice.

The first and second methods are simpler and less costly, and therefore are recommended over the third for persons who wish to operate the corporation anonymously.

DEDUCTION OF CORPORATE STOCK
LOSS FROM PERSONAL INCOME

SECTION XVII

A valuable tax law exists that is beneficial to shareholders of a corporation.

Section 1244 of the Internal Revenue Code enables a shareholder to deduct certain losses in investment of stock as ordinary income losses. Experienced tax lawyers sometimes advise their clients of the existence of this tax law.

Under Section 1244 and subject to its conditions, if a shareholder in a corporation (shareholder can be any individual or partnership, but not a corporation, estate or trust) incurs a loss through sale of his or her stock or if the stock becomes worthless, this section allows a deduction of the loss up to $50,000 a year ($100,000 on a joint return) from personal income. Normally, a loss on a stock investment is subject to special capital loss limitations under the Internal Revenue Code. There are no disadvantages in qualifying the corporation under Section 1244 if the corporation is eligible, as most small ones are. The potential tax benefits are well worth it, and shareholders have nothing to lose. Also, more investors are potentially attracted to purchasing stock in a corporation when made aware of the Section 1244 provision. Of course, a person should always be cautious in how and to whom stock in a corporation is offered so that federal regulations under the Securities Act of 1933 are not violated. This legal arrangement of qualifying a corporation under Section 1244 can be put into effect upon the formation of the corporation by completing simple forms. Nothing has to be filed with the Internal Revenue Service. A copy of the Internal Revenue Code Section 1244 is on the following page. One registered agent service company, The Company Corporation, provides standard forms to all clients as a standard part of its service. (See Section VIII.)

NOTE: Every Subchapter S corporation (see Section XVIII) should qualify under Section 1244. Subchapter S and Section 1244 complement each other in the tax advantages they provide. Operating losses of an S corporation may be passed on to the shareholders currently, whereas a loss in value in the assets of a Section 1244 corporation can be taken as an ordinary loss on the sale and exchange of stock.

SECTION 1244. LOSSES ON SMALL BUSINESS STOCK.

(a) GENERAL RULE.—In the case of an individual, a loss on section 1244 stock issued to such individual or to a partnership which would (but for this section) be treated as a loss from the sale or exchange of a capital asset shall, to the extent provided in this section, be treated as an ordinary loss.

(b) MAXIMUM AMOUNT FOR ANY TAXABLE YEAR.—For any taxable year the aggregate amount treated by the taxpayers by reason of this section as an ordinary loss shall not exceed—

    (1) $50,000 or

    (2) $100,000 in the case of a husband and wife filing a joint return for such year under section 6013.

(c) SECTION 1244 STOCK DEFINED.—

    (1) IN GENERAL.—For purposes of this section, the term "section 1244 stock" means common stock in a domestic corporation if—

        (A) at the time such stock is issued, such corporation was a small business corporation,

        (B) such stock was issued by such corporation for money or other property (other than stock and securities), and

        (C) such corporation, during the period of its 5 most recent taxable years ending before the date and loss on such stock was sustained, derived more than 50 percent of its aggregate gross receipts from sources other than royalties, rents, dividends, interests, annuities, and sales or exchanges of stocks or securities.

    (2) RULES FOR APPLICATION OF PARAGRAPH (1)(C).—

        (A) Period taken into account with respect to new corporations.—For purposes of paragraph (1)(C), if the corporation has not been in existence for 5 taxable years ending before the date the loss on the stock was sustained, there shall be substituted for such 5-year period—

            (i) the period of the corporation's taxable years ending before such date, or

            (ii) if the corporation has not been in existence for 1 taxable year ending before such date, the period such corporation has been in existence before such date.

        (B) Gross receipts from sales of securities.—For purposes of paragraph (1)(C), gross receipts from the sales or exchanges of stock or securities shall be taken into account only to the extent of gains therefrom.

        (C) Nonapplication where deductions exceed gross income.—Paragraph (1)(C) shall not apply with respect to any corporation if, for the period taken into account for purposes of paragraph (1)(C), the amount of the deductions allowed by this chapter (other than by sections 172, 243, 244, and 245) exceeds the amount of gross income.

    (3) SMALL BUSINESS CORPORATION DEFINED.—

        (A) In general.—For purposes of this section, a corporation shall be treated as a small business corporation if the aggregate amount of money and other property received by the corporation for stock, as a contribution to capital, and as paid-in surplus, does not exceed $1,000,000. The determination under the preceding sentence shall be made as of the time of the issuance of the stock in question but shall include amounts received for such stock and for all stock theretofore issued.

        (B) Amount taken into account with respect to property.—For purposes of subparagraph (A), the amount taken into account with respect to any property other than money shall be the amount equal to the adjusted basis to the corporation of such property for determining gain, reduced by any liability to which the property was subject or which was assumed by the corporation. The determination under the preceding sentence shall be made as of the time the property was received by the corporation.

(d) SPECIAL RULES.—

    (1) LIMITATIONS ON AMOUNT OF ORDINARY LOSS.—

        (A) Contributions of property having basis in excess of value.—If—

            (i) section 1244 stock was issued in exchange for property.

            (ii) the basis of such stock in the hands of the taxpayer is determined by reference to the basis in his hands of such property, and

            (iii) the adjusted basis (for determining loss) of such property immediately before the exchange exceeded its fair market value at such time, then in computing the amount of the loss on such stock for purposes of this section the basis of such stock shall be reduced by an amount equal to the excess described in clause (iii).

        (B) Increases in basis.—In computing the amount of the loss on stock for purposes of this section, any increase in the basis of such stock (through contributions to the capital of the corporation, or otherwise) shall be treated as allocable to stock which is not section 1244 stock.

    (2) RECAPITALIZATION, CHANGES IN NAME, ETC.—To the extent provided in regulations prescribed by the Secretary, common stock in a corporation, the basis of which (in the hands of a taxpayer) is determined in whole or in part by reference to the basis in his hands of stock in such corporation which meets the requirements of sub-section (c)(1) (other than subparagraph (C) thereof), or which is received in a reorganization described in section 368(a)(1)(F) in exchange for stock which meets such requirements, shall be treated as meeting such requirements. For purposes of paragraphs (1)(C) and (3)(A) of subsection (c), a successor corporation in a reorganization described in section 368(a)(1)(F) shall be treated as the same corporation as its predecessor.

    (3) RELATIONSHIP TO NET OPERATING LOSS DEDUCTION.—For purposes of section 172 (relating to the net operating loss deduction), any amount of loss treated by reason of this section as an ordinary loss shall be treated as attributable to a trade or business of the taxpayer.

    (4) INDIVIDUAL DEFINED.—For purposes of this section, the term individual does not include a trust or estate.

(e) REGULATIONS.—The Secretary shall prescribe such regulations as may be necessary to carry out the purposes of this section.

S CORPORATION—BENEFITS OF CORPORATIONS TAXED AS A PROPRIETORSHIP OR PARTNERSHIP

SECTION XVIII

Forming an S corporation makes possible the best of all worlds—the benefits of incorporation with only a single tax at individual rates.

A corporation ordinarily pays tax on its profits at corporate rates. Tax is again owed—this time by shareholders—when dividends are paid.

Fortunately, this double taxation can easily be completely eliminated by bringing your corporation under the S corporation status. As an S corporation, earnings are taxed only once. Rather than being taxed to the corporation, profits are included in your personal return and taxed at your individual rates.

If an S corporation has a loss for the year, the loss is passed directly to your tax return and thus reduces your personal tax bill. Losses of a regular C corporation must be retained in the business for a possible later offset against corporate earnings. Shareholders receive no immediate benefit.

S corporation tax breaks are available without loss of limited liability, easy transferability of stock and other advantages available only to a corporation.

A person may call any Internal Revenue office and obtain Form 2553.* This is a one-page form that permits tax filing as an S corporation. Corporations eligible to elect this tax status must meet five simple requirements. The following is a quotation from Form 2553:

Corporations eligible to elect.—The election may be made only if the corporation is a domestic corporation which meets all eight of the following requirements:

1. It is a domestic corporation.

2. It has no more than 35 shareholders. A husband and wife (and their estates) are treated as one shareholder for this requirement. All other persons are treated as separate shareholders.

3. It has only individuals, estates or certain trusts as shareholders.

4. It has no nonresident alien shareholders.

5. It has only one class of stock (disregarding differences in voting rights). Generally, a corporation is treated as having only one class of stock if all outstanding shares of the corporation's stock confer identical rights to distribution and liquidation proceeds.

6. It is not one of the following ineligible corporations:

    a. a corporation that owns 80 percent or more of the stock of another corporation, unless the other corporation has not begun business and has no gross income;

    b. a bank or thrift institution;

    c. an insurance company subject to tax under the special rules of Subchapter L of the Internal Revenue Code;

    d. a corporation that has elected to be treated as a possessions corporation under section 936; or

    e. a domestic international sales corporation (DISC) or former DISC.

---

* The Company Corporation can obtain S status for your corporation for the nominal fee of $35.

59

7. It has a permitted tax year as required by section 1378 or makes a section 444 election to have a tax year other than a permitted tax year. Section 1378 defines a permitted tax year as a tax year ending December 31, or any other tax year for which the corporation establishes a business purpose to the satisfaction of the IRS.

8. Each shareholder consents as explained in the instructions for Column K (See IRS Form 2553).

A complete set of forms for filing for S corporation status is included in this chapter or can be obtained from any IRS office. These forms can be completed without professional help. However, any good accountant can assist in completing this form if desired. The Company Corporation can provide assistance for a fee of $35.

Department of the Treasury
Internal Revenue Service

Instructions for Form 2553
(Revised September 1993)

Election by a Small Business Corporation

Section references are to the Internal Revenue Code unless otherwise noted.

Paperwork Reduction Act Notice.—We ask for the information on this form to carry out the Internal Revenue laws of the United States. You are required to give us the information. We need it to ensure that you are complying with these laws and to allow us to figure and collect the right amount of tax.

The time needed to complete and file this form will vary depending on individual circumstances. The estimated average time is:

Recordkeeping . . . . . 6 hr., 13 min.

Learning about the law or the form . . . . . 2 hr., 59 min.

Preparing, copying, assembling, and sending the form to the IRS . . . 3 hr., 13 min.

If you have comments concerning the accuracy of these time estimates or suggestions for making this form more simple, we would be happy to hear from you. You can write to both the **Internal Revenue Service,** Attention: Reports Clearance Officer, T:FP, Washington, DC 20224; and the **Office of Management and Budget,** Paperwork Reduction Project (1545-0146), Washington, DC 20503. **DO NOT** send the tax form to either of these offices. Instead, see **Where To File** below.

General Instructions

Purpose.—To elect to be an "S corporation," a corporation must file Form 2553. The election permits the income of the S corporation to be taxed to the shareholders of the corporation rather than to the corporation itself, except as provided in Subchapter S of the Code. For more information, get **Pub. 589,** Tax Information on S Corporations.

Who May Elect.—A corporation may elect to be an S corporation only if it meets **all** of the following tests:

1. It is a domestic corporation.

2. it has no more than 35 shareholders. A husband and wife (and their estates) are treated as one shareholder for this requirement. All other persons are treated as separate shareholders.

3. It has only individuals, estates, or certain trusts as shareholders. See the instructions for Part III regarding qualified subchapter S trusts.

4. It has no nonresident alien shareholders.

5. It has only one class of stock (disregarding differences in voting rights). Generally, a corporation is treated as having only one class of stock if all outstanding shares of the corporation's stock confer identical rights to distribution and liquidation

proceeds. See Regulations section 1.1361-1(l) for more details.

6. It is not one of the following ineligible corporations:

a. A corporation that owns 80% or more of the stock of another corporation, unless the other corporation has not begun business and has no gross income;

b. A bank or thrift institution;

c. An insurance company subject to tax under the special rules of Subchapter L of the Code;

d. A corporation that has elected to be treated as a possessions corporation under section 936; or

e. A domestic international sales corporation (DISC) or former DISC.

7. It has a permitted tax year as required by section 1378 or makes a section 444 election to have a tax year other than a permitted tax year. Section 1378 defines a permitted tax year as a tax year ending December 31, or any other tax year for which the corporation establishes a business purpose to the satisfaction of the IRS. See Part II for details on requesting a fiscal tax year based on a business purpose or on making a section 444 election.

8. Each shareholder consents as explained in the instructions for Column K.

See sections 1361, 1362, and 1378 for additional information on the above tests.

Where To File.—File this election with the Internal Revenue Service Center listed below.

If the corporation's principal business, office, or agency is located in ▼	Use the following Internal Revenue Service Center address ▼
New Jersey, New York (New York City and counties of Nassau, Rockland, Suffolk, and Westchester)	Holtsville, NY 00501
New York (all other counties), Connecticut, Maine, Massachusetts, New Hampshire, Rhode Island, Vermont	Andover, MA 05501
Illinois, Iowa, Minnesota, Missouri, Wisconsin	Kansas City, MO 64999
Delaware, District of Columbia, Maryland, Pennsylvania, Virginia	Philadelphia, PA 19255
Florida, Georgia, South Carolina	Atlanta, GA 39901
Indiana, Kentucky, Michigan, Ohio, West Virginia	Cincinnati, OH 45999
Kansas, New Mexico, Oklahoma, Texas	Austin, TX 73301
Alaska, Arizona, California (counties of Alpine, Amador, Butte, Calaveras, Colusa, Contra Costa, Del Norte, El Dorado, Glenn, Humboldt, Lake, Lassen, Marin, Mendocino, Modoc, Napa, Nevada, Placer, Plumas, Sacramento, San Joaquin, Shasta, Sierra, Siskiyou, Solano, Sonoma, Sutter, Tehama, Trinity, Yolo, and Yuba), Colorado, Idaho, Montana, Nebraska, Nevada, North Dakota, Oregon, South Dakota, Utah, Washington, Wyoming	Ogden, UT 84201
California (all other counties), Hawaii	Fresno, CA 93888
Alabama, Arkansas, Louisiana, Mississippi, North Carolina, Tennessee	Memphis, TN 37501

When To Make the Election.—Complete and file Form 2553 **(a)** at any time before the 16th day of the third month of the tax year, if filed during the tax year the election is to take effect, or **(b)** at any time during the preceding tax year. An election made no later than 2 months and 15 days after the beginning of a tax year that is less than 2½ months long is treated as timely made for that tax year. An election made after the 15th day of the third month but before the end of the tax year is effective for the next year. For example, if a calendar tax year corporation makes the election in April 1994, it is effective for the corporation's 1995 calendar tax year. See section 1362(b) for more information.

Acceptance or Nonacceptance of Election.—The Service Center will notify the corporation if its election is accepted and when it will take effect. The corporation will also be notified if its election is not accepted. The corporation should generally receive a determination on its election within 60 days after it has filed Form 2553. If box Q1 in Part II is checked on page 2, the corporation will receive a ruling letter from the IRS in Washington, DC, that either approves or denies the selected tax year. When box Q1 is checked, it will generally take an additional 90 days for the Form 2553 to be accepted.

Do not file Form 1120S until the corporation is notified that its election has been accepted. If the corporation is now required to file **Form 1120,** U.S. Corporation Income Tax Return, or any other applicable tax return, continue filing it until the election takes effect.

Care should be exercised to ensure that the IRS receives the election. If the corporation is not notified of acceptance or nonacceptance of its election within 3 months

Cat. No. 49978N

of date of filing (date mailed), or within 6 months if box Q1 is checked, please take follow-up action by corresponding with the Service Center where the corporation filed the election. If the IRS questions whether Form 2553 was filed, an acceptable proof of filing is: **(a)** certified or registered mail receipt (timely filed); **(b)** Form 2553 with accepted stamp; **(c)** Form 2553 with stamped IRS received date; or **(d)** IRS letter stating that Form 2553 has been accepted.

End of Election.— Once the election is made, it stays in effect for all years until it is terminated. During the 5 years after the election is terminated under section 1362(d), the corporation (or a successor corporation) can make another election on Form 2553 only with IRS consent. See Regulations section 1.1362-5 for more details.

Specific Instructions
Part I

Part I must be completed by all corporations.

Name and Address of Corporation.—Enter the true corporate name as set forth in the corporate charter or other legal document creating it. If the corporation's mailing address is the same as someone else's, such as a shareholder's, please enter "c/o" and this person's name following the name of the corporation. Include the suite, room, or other unit number after the street address. If the Post Office does not deliver to the street address and the corporation has a P.O. box, show the box number instead of the street address. If the corporation changed its name or address after applying for its EIN, be sure to check the box in item G of Part I.

Item A. Employer Identification Number.—If the corporation has applied for an employer identification number (EIN) but has not received it, enter "applied for." If the corporation does not have an EIN, it should apply for one on **Form SS-4,** Application for Employer Identification Number, available from most IRS and Social Security Administration offices.

Item D. Effective Date of Election.—Enter the beginning effective date (month, day, year) of the tax year requested for the S corporation. Generally, this will be the beginning date of the tax year for which the ending effective date is required to be shown in item I, Part I. For a new corporation (first year the corporation exists) it will generally be the date required to be shown in item H, Part I. The tax year of a new corporation starts on the date that it has shareholders, acquires assets, or begins doing business, whichever happens first. If the effective date for item D for a newly formed corporation is later than the date in item H, the corporation should file Form 1120 or Form 1120-A, for the tax period between these dates.

Column K. Shareholders' Consent Statement.—Each shareholder who owns (or is deemed to own) stock at the time the election is made must consent to the election. If the election is made during the corporation's tax year for which it first takes effect, any person who held stock at any time during the part of that year that occurs before the election is made, must consent to the election, even though the person may have sold or transferred his or her stock before the

election is made. Each shareholder consents by signing and dating in column K or signing and dating a separate consent statement described below.

An election made during the first 2½ months of the tax year is effective for the following tax year if any person who held stock in the corporation during the part of the tax year before the election was made, and who did not hold stock at the time the election was made, did not consent to the election.

If a husband and wife have a community interest in the stock or in the income from it, both must consent. Each tenant in common, joint tenant, and tenant by the entirety also must consent.

A minor's consent is made by the minor or the legal representative of the minor, or by a natural or adoptive parent of the minor if no legal representative has been appointed.

The consent of an estate is made by an executor or administrator.

If stock is owned by a trust that is a qualified shareholder, the deemed owner of the trust must consent. See section 1361(c)(2) for details regarding qualified trusts that may be shareholders and rules on determining who is the deemed owner of the trust.

Continuation sheet or separate consent statement.—If you need a continuation sheet or use a separate consent statement, attach it to Form 2553. The separate consent statement must contain the name, address, and employer identification number of the corporation and the shareholder information requested in columns J through N of Part I.

If you want, you may combine all the shareholders' consents in one statement.

Column L.—Enter the number of shares of stock each shareholder owns and the dates the stock was acquired. If the election is made during the corporation's tax year for which it first takes effect, do not list the shares of stock for those shareholders who sold or transferred all of their stock before the election was made. However, these shareholders must still consent to the election for it to be effective for the tax year.

Column M.—Enter the social security number of each shareholder who is an individual. Enter the employer identification number of each shareholder that is an estate or a qualified trust.

Column N.—Enter the month and day that each shareholder's tax year ends. If a shareholder is changing his or her tax year, enter the tax year the shareholder is changing to, and attach an explanation indicating the present tax year and the basis for the change (e.g., automatic revenue procedure or letter ruling request).

If the election is made during the corporation's tax year for which it first takes effect, you do not have to enter the tax year of any shareholder who sold or transferred all of his or her stock before the election was made.

Signature.—Form 2553 must be signed by the president, treasurer, assistant treasurer, chief accounting officer, or other corporate officer (such as tax officer) authorized to sign.

Part II

Complete Part II if you selected a tax year ending on any date other than December 31

(other than a 52-53-week tax year ending with reference to the month of December).

Box P1.—Attach a statement showing separately for each month the amount of gross receipts for the most recent 47 months as required by section 4.03(3) of Revenue Procedure 87-32, 1987-2 C.B. 396. A corporation that does not have a 47-month period of gross receipts cannot establish a natural business year under section 4.01(1).

Box Q1.—For examples of an acceptable business purpose for requesting a fiscal tax year, see Revenue Ruling 87-57, 1987-2 C.B. 117.

In addition to a statement showing the business purpose for the requested fiscal year, you must attach the other information necessary to meet the ruling request requirements of Revenue Procedure 93-1, 1993-1 I.R.B. 10 (updated annually). Also attach a statement that shows separately the amount of gross receipts from sales or services (and inventory costs, if applicable) for each of the 36 months preceding the effective date of the election to be an S corporation. If the corporation has been in existence for fewer than 36 months, submit figures for the period of existence.

If you check box Q1, you must also pay a user fee of $200 (subject to change). Do not pay the fee when filing Form 2553. The Service Center will send Form 2553 to the IRS in Washington, DC, who, in turn, will notify the corporation that the fee is due. See Revenue Procedure 93-23, 1993-19 I.R.B. 6.

Box Q2.—If the corporation makes a back-up section 444 election for which it is qualified, then the election must be exercised in the event the business purpose request is not approved. Under certain circumstances, the tax year requested under the back-up section 444 election may be different than the tax year requested under business purpose. See **Form 8716,** Election To Have a Tax Year Other Than a Required Tax Year, for details on making a back-up section 444 election.

Boxes Q2 and R2.—If the corporation is not qualified to make the section 444 election after making the item Q2 back-up section 444 election or indicating its intention to make the election in item R1, and therefore it later files a calendar year return, it should write "Section 444 Election Not Made" in the top left corner of the 1st calendar year Form 1120S it files.

Part III

Certain Qualified Subchapter S Trusts (QSSTs) may make the QSST election required by section 1361(d)(2) in Part III. Part III may be used to make the QSST election only if corporate stock has been transferred to the trust on or before the date on which the corporation makes its election to be an S corporation. However, a statement can be used in lieu of Part III to make the election.

Note: *Part III may be used only in conjunction with making the Part I election (i.e., Form 2553 cannot be filed with only Part III completed).*

The deemed owner of the QSST must also consent to the S corporation election in column K, page 1, of Form 2553. See section 1361(c)(2).

Page 2

♻ *Printed on recycled paper*

*U.S. Government Printing Office: 1993 — 301-628/80272

Form **2553**
(Rev. September 1993)

Department of the Treasury
Internal Revenue Service

Election by a Small Business Corporation
(Under section 1362 of the Internal Revenue Code)
▶ For Paperwork Reduction Act Notice, see page 1 of instructions.
▶ See separate instructions.

OMB No. 1545-0146
Expires 8-31-96

Notes: 1. This election, to be an "S corporation," can be accepted only if all the tests are met under **Who May Elect** on page 1 of the instructions; all signatures in Parts I and III are originals (no photocopies); and the exact name and address of the corporation and other required form information are provided.

2. Do not file **Form 1120S**, U.S. Income Tax Return for an S Corporation, until you are notified that your election is accepted.

Part I	**Election Information**	

Please Type or Print

Name of corporation (see instructions)	**A** Employer identification number (EIN)
ABC Corporation	52 : 3657893
Number, street, and room or suite no. (If a P.O. box, see instructions.)	**B** Date incorporated
1 Main Street	Jan. 2, 1996
City or town, state, and ZIP code	**C** State of incorporation
New City, NY 10005	DE

D Election is to be effective for tax year beginning (month, day, year) . . . . ▶Jan / 2 / 1996

E Name and title of officer or legal representative who the IRS may call for more information

John Smith, President

F Telephone number of officer or legal representative
(212) 555-5555

G If the corporation changed its name or address after applying for the EIN shown in **A**, check this box . . . . ▶ ☐

H If this election takes effect for the first tax year the corporation exists, enter month, day, and year of the **earliest** of the following: (1) date the corporation first had shareholders, (2) date the corporation first had assets, or (3) date the corporation began doing business . . . . ▶ Jan / 2 / 1996

I Selected tax year: Annual return will be filed for tax year ending (month and day) ▶ . . . .

If the tax year ends on any date other than December 31, except for an automatic 52-53-week tax year ending with reference to the month of December, you **must** complete Part II on the back. If the date you enter is the ending date of an automatic 52-53-week tax year, write "52-53-week year" to the right of the date. See Temporary Regulations section 1.441-2T(e)(3).

J Name and address of each shareholder, shareholder's spouse having a community property interest in the corporation's stock, and each tenant in common, joint tenant, and tenant by the entirety. (A husband and wife (and their estates) are counted as one shareholder in determining the number of shareholders without regard to the manner in which the stock is owned.)	**K** Shareholders' Consent Statement. Under penalties of perjury, we declare that we consent to the election of the above-named corporation to be an "S corporation" under section 1362(a) and that we have examined this consent statement, including accompanying schedules and statements, and to the best of our knowledge and belief, it is true, correct, and complete. (Shareholders sign and date below.)*		**L** Stock owned		**M** Social security number or employer identification number (see instructions)	**N** Shareholder's tax year ends (month and day)
	Signature	Date	Number of shares	Dates acquired		
John Smith	*John Smith*	1/2/96	20	1/2/96	222-88-5555	Dec. 31
Joan James	*Joan James*	1/2/96	20	1/2/96	222-55-8888	Dec. 31
Ken Brown	*Ken Brown*	1/2/96	20	1/2/96	222-77-6666	Dec. 31
Ann Green	*Ann Green*	1/2/96	20	1/2/96	222-66-3333	Dec. 31
Bart Black	*Bart Black*	1/2/96	20	1/2/96	222-11-9999	Dec. 31

*For this election to be valid, the consent of each shareholder, shareholder's spouse having a community property interest in the corporation's stock, and each tenant in common, joint tenant, and tenant by the entirety must either appear above or be attached to this form. (See instructions for Column K if a continuation sheet or a separate consent statement is needed.)

Under penalties of perjury, I declare that I have examined this election, including accompanying schedules and statements, and to the best of my knowledge and belief, it is true, correct, and complete.

Signature of officer ▶ *John Smith* Title ▶ President Date ▶ 1/3/96

See Parts II and III on back.   Cat. No. 18629R   Form **2553** (Rev. 9-93)

Part II Selection of Fiscal Tax Year (All corporations using this part must complete item O and one of items P, Q, or R.)

O Check the applicable box below to indicate whether the corporation is:

  1. ☐ A new corporation adopting the tax year entered in item I, Part I.

  2. ☐ An existing corporation retaining the tax year entered in item I, Part I.

  3. ☐ An existing corporation changing to the tax year entered in item I, Part I.

P Complete item P if the corporation is using the expeditious approval provisions of Revenue Procedure 87-32, 1987-2 C.B. 396, to request: **(1)** a natural business year (as defined in section 4.01(1) of Rev. Proc. 87-32), or **(2)** a year that satisfies the ownership tax year test in section 4.01(2) of Rev. Proc. 87-32. Check the applicable box below to indicate the representation statement the corporation is making as required under section 4 of Rev. Proc. 87-32.

  1. Natural Business Year ▶ ☐ I represent that the corporation is retaining or changing to a tax year that coincides with its natural business year as defined in section 4.01(1) of Rev. Proc. 87-32 and as verified by its satisfaction of the requirements of section 4.02(1) of Rev. Proc. 87-32. In addition, if the corporation is changing to a natural business year as defined in section 4.01(1), I further represent that such tax year results in less deferral of income to the owners than the corporation's present tax year. I also represent that the corporation is not described in section 3.01(2) of Rev. Proc. 87-32. (See instructions for additional information that must be attached.)

  2. Ownership Tax Year ▶ ☐ I represent that shareholders holding more than half of the shares of the stock (as of the first day of the tax year to which the request relates) of the corporation have the same tax year or are concurrently changing to the tax year that the corporation adopts, retains, or changes to per item I, Part I. I also represent that the corporation is not described in section 3.01(2) of Rev. Proc. 87-32.

Note: *If you do not use item P and the corporation wants a fiscal tax year, complete either item Q or R below. Item Q is used to request a fiscal tax year based on a business purpose and to make a back-up section 444 election. Item R is used to make a regular section 444 election.*

Q Business Purpose—To request a fiscal tax year based on a business purpose, you must check box Q1 and pay a user fee. See instructions for details. You may also check box Q2 and/or box Q3.

  1. Check here ▶ ☐ if the fiscal year entered in item I, Part I, is requested under the provisions of section 6.03 of Rev. Proc. 87-32. Attach to Form 2553 a statement showing the business purpose for the requested fiscal year. See instructions for additional information that must be attached.

  2. Check here ▶ ☐ to show that the corporation intends to make a back-up section 444 election in the event the corporation's business purpose request is not approved by the IRS. (See instructions for more information.)

  3. Check here ▶ ☐ to show that the corporation agrees to adopt or change to a tax year ending December 31 if necessary for the IRS to accept this election for S corporation status in the event: (1) the corporation's business purpose request is not approved and the corporation makes a back-up section 444 election, but is ultimately not qualified to make a section 444 election, or (2) the corporation's business purpose request is not approved and the corporation did not make a back-up section 444 election.

R Section 444 Election—To make a section 444 election, you must check box R1 and you may also check box R2.

  1. Check here ▶ ☐ to show the corporation will make, if qualified, a section 444 election to have the fiscal tax year shown in item I, Part I. To make the election, you must complete **Form 8716,** Election To Have a Tax Year Other Than a Required Tax Year, and either attach it to Form 2553 or file it separately.

  2. Check here ▶ ☐ to show that the corporation agrees to adopt or change to a tax year ending December 31 if necessary for the IRS to accept this election for S corporation status in the event the corporation is ultimately not qualified to make a section 444 election.

Part III Qualified Subchapter S Trust (QSST) Election Under Section 1361(d)(2)**

Income beneficiary's name and address	Social security number
Trust's name and address	Employer identification number

Date on which stock of the corporation was transferred to the trust (month, day, year) . . . . ▶   /   /

In order for the trust named above to be a QSST and thus a qualifying shareholder of the S corporation for which this Form 2553 is filed, I hereby make the election under section 1361(d)(2). Under penalties of perjury, I certify that the trust meets the definitional requirements of section 1361(d)(3) and that all other information provided in Part III is true, correct, and complete.

_____   _____
Signature of income beneficiary or signature and title of legal representative or other qualified person making the election   Date

**Use of Part III to make the QSST election may be made only if stock of the corporation has been transferred to the trust on or before the date on which the corporation makes its election to be an S corporation. The QSST election must be made and filed separately if stock of the corporation is transferred to the trust after the date on which the corporation makes the S election.

✪ *Printed on recycled paper*   *U.S. Government Printing Office: 1993 — 301-628/80271

64

Form **2553**
(Rev. September 1993)

Department of the Treasury
Internal Revenue Service

Election by a Small Business Corporation
(Under section 1362 of the Internal Revenue Code)
▶ For Paperwork Reduction Act Notice, see page 1 of instructions.
▶ See separate instructions.

OMB No. 1545-0146
Expires 8-31-96

Notes:
1. This election, to be an "S corporation," can be accepted only if all the tests are met under **Who May Elect** on page 1 of the instructions; all signatures in Parts I and III are originals (no photocopies); and the exact name and address of the corporation and other required form information are provided.
2. Do not file **Form 1120S**, U.S. Income Tax Return for an S Corporation, until you are notified that your election is accepted.

Part I Election Information

Please Type or Print

Name of corporation (see instructions)	**A** Employer identification number (EIN)
Number, street, and room or suite no. (If a P.O. box, see instructions.)	**B** Date incorporated
City or town, state, and ZIP code	**C** State of incorporation

D Election is to be effective for tax year beginning (month, day, year) . . . . ▶ / /

E Name and title of officer or legal representative who the IRS may call for more information

F Telephone number of officer or legal representative ( )

G If the corporation changed its name or address after applying for the EIN shown in **A,** check this box . . . . ▶ ☐

H If this election takes effect for the first tax year the corporation exists, enter month, day, and year of the **earliest** of the following: (1) date the corporation first had shareholders, (2) date the corporation first had assets, or (3) date the corporation began doing business . . . . ▶ / /

I Selected tax year: Annual return will be filed for tax year ending (month and day) ▶ . . . .

If the tax year ends on any date other than December 31, except for an automatic 52-53-week tax year ending with reference to the month of December, you **must** complete Part II on the back. If the date you enter is the ending date of an automatic 52-53-week tax year, write "52-53-week year" to the right of the date. See Temporary Regulations section 1.441-2T(e)(3).

J Name and address of each shareholder, shareholder's spouse having a community property interest in the corporation's stock, and each tenant in common, joint tenant, and tenant by the entirety. (A husband and wife (and their estates) are counted as one shareholder in determining the number of shareholders without regard to the manner in which the stock is owned.)	**K** Shareholders' Consent Statement. Under penalties of perjury, we declare that we consent to the election of the above-named corporation to be an "S corporation" under section 1362(a) and that we have examined this consent statement, including accompanying schedules and statements, and to the best of our knowledge and belief, it is true, correct, and complete. (Shareholders sign and date below.)*		**L** Stock owned		**M** Social security number or employer identification number (see instructions)	**N** Share-holder's tax year ends (month and day)
	Signature	Date	Number of shares	Dates acquired		

*For this election to be valid, the consent of each shareholder, shareholder's spouse having a community property interest in the corporation's stock, and each tenant in common, joint tenant, and tenant by the entirety must either appear above or be attached to this form. (See instructions for Column K if a continuation sheet or a separate consent statement is needed.)

Under penalties of perjury, I declare that I have examined this election, including accompanying schedules and statements, and to the best of my knowledge and belief, it is true, correct, and complete.

Signature of officer ▶   Title ▶   Date ▶

See Parts II and III on back.   Cat. No. 18629R   Form **2553** (Rev. 9-93)

Part II	Selection of Fiscal Tax Year (All corporations using this part must complete item O and one of items P, Q, or R.)

O Check the applicable box below to indicate whether the corporation is:

1. ☐ A new corporation adopting the tax year entered in item I, Part I.
2. ☐ An existing corporation retaining the tax year entered in item I, Part I.
3. ☐ An existing corporation changing to the tax year entered in item I, Part I.

P Complete item P if the corporation is using the expeditious approval provisions of Revenue Procedure 87-32, 1987-2 C.B. 396, to request: **(1)** a natural business year (as defined in section 4.01(1) of Rev. Proc. 87-32), or **(2)** a year that satisfies the ownership tax year test in section 4.01(2) of Rev. Proc. 87-32. Check the applicable box below to indicate the representation statement the corporation is making as required under section 4 of Rev. Proc. 87-32.

1. **Natural Business Year** ► ☐ I represent that the corporation is retaining or changing to a tax year that coincides with its natural business year as defined in section 4.01(1) of Rev. Proc. 87-32 and as verified by its satisfaction of the requirements of section 4.02(1) of Rev. Proc. 87-32. In addition, if the corporation is changing to a natural business year as defined in section 4.01(1), I further represent that such tax year results in less deferral of income to the owners than the corporation's present tax year. I also represent that the corporation is not described in section 3.01(2) of Rev. Proc. 87-32. (See instructions for additional information that must be attached.)

2. **Ownership Tax Year** ► ☐ I represent that shareholders holding more than half of the shares of the stock (as of the first day of the tax year to which the request relates) of the corporation have the same tax year or are concurrently changing to the tax year that the corporation adopts, retains, or changes to per item I, Part I. I also represent that the corporation is not described in section 3.01(2) of Rev. Proc. 87-32.

Note: *If you do not use item P and the corporation wants a fiscal tax year, complete either item Q or R below. Item Q is used to request a fiscal tax year based on a business purpose and to make a back-up section 444 election. Item R is used to make a regular section 444 election.*

Q Business Purpose—To request a fiscal tax year based on a business purpose, you must check box Q1 and pay a user fee. See instructions for details. You may also check box Q2 and/or box Q3.

1. **Check here** ► ☐ if the fiscal year entered in item I, Part I, is requested under the provisions of section 6.03 of Rev. Proc. 87-32. Attach to Form 2553 a statement showing the business purpose for the requested fiscal year. See instructions for additional information that must be attached.

2. **Check here** ► ☐ to show that the corporation intends to make a back-up section 444 election in the event the corporation's business purpose request is not approved by the IRS. (See instructions for more information.)

3. **Check here** ► ☐ to show that the corporation agrees to adopt or change to a tax year ending December 31 if necessary for the IRS to accept this election for S corporation status in the event: (1) the corporation's business purpose request is not approved and the corporation makes a back-up section 444 election, but is ultimately not qualified to make a section 444 election, or (2) the corporation's business purpose request is not approved and the corporation did not make a back-up section 444 election.

R Section 444 Election—To make a section 444 election, you must check box R1 and you may also check box R2.

1. **Check here** ► ☐ to show the corporation will make, if qualified, a section 444 election to have the fiscal tax year shown in item I, Part I. To make the election, you must complete **Form 8716,** Election To Have a Tax Year Other Than a Required Tax Year, and either attach it to Form 2553 or file it separately.

2. **Check here** ► ☐ to show that the corporation agrees to adopt or change to a tax year ending December 31 if necessary for the IRS to accept this election for S corporation status in the event the corporation is ultimately not qualified to make a section 444 election.

Part III	Qualified Subchapter S Trust (QSST) Election Under Section 1361(d)(2)**

Income beneficiary's name and address	Social security number
Trust's name and address	Employer identification number

Date on which stock of the corporation was transferred to the trust (month, day, year) . . . . ► / /

In order for the trust named above to be a QSST and thus a qualifying shareholder of the S corporation for which this Form 2553 is filed, I hereby make the election under section 1361(d)(2). Under penalties of perjury, I certify that the trust meets the definitional requirements of section 1361(d)(3) and that all other information provided in Part III is true, correct, and complete.

_____ _____
Signature of income beneficiary or signature and title of legal representative or other qualified person making the election   Date

**Use of Part III to make the QSST election may be made only if stock of the corporation has been transferred to the trust on or before the date on which the corporation makes its election to be an S corporation. The QSST election must be made and filed separately if stock of the corporation is transferred to the trust after the date on which the corporation makes the S election.

✸ *Printed on recycled paper*   *U.S. Government Printing Office: 1993 — 301-628/80271

66

NONPROFIT CORPORATIONS

SECTION XIX

A nonprofit corporation is a special type of corporation formed for charitable or other purposes that are not profit seeking. It has many of the features of standard corporations with the major exception being its tax status.

The number of nonprofit corporations in the United States is remarkable, running into the hundreds of thousands. In some states like Ohio and New York, over one-third of all corporations chartered are nonprofit. While there are critics of the growing phenomenon of the nonprofit corporation, over 50 percent of the property in some towns and cities is tax-exempt. Real property of certain organizations is wholly exempt from real property taxation (e.g., churches, colleges, etc.). However, as long as the minimal requirements of the IRS are met, it is legal under existing law, and the nonprofit corporation is likely to keep expanding and growing.

Nonprofit corporations do not issue stock. Instead, membership certificates are often used. The form for a nonstock, nonprofit corporation that is recommended for use is on the following page. It can be completed in the same way as the earlier certificates in this book and either mailed directly to the appropriate Secretary of State or through a registered agent.

Some individuals utilize nonprofit corporations as a tax shelter. Many corporate situations lend themselves to this tax-exempt status. These endeavors can provide desirable tax advantages to the owner(s) of a corporation that may qualify for a government grant to do research, educational experiments and the like.

A corporation can often qualify for tax-exempt status and still pay its officers' salaries and expenses. The Internal Revenue Service may question these salaries and expenses on a tax audit, however, if they are excessive.

Other situations lending themselves to nonprofit status are religious, fraternal and civic clubs. Neighborhood associations, too, often incorporate as nonprofit corporations, primarily to gain personal liability protection for their members. Still another example is when a person or group creates a nonprofit foundation for charitable purposes, such as medical research.

Often a person's will can be worded to leave such assets as stockholdings or insurance proceeds (by insurance contract) to a nonprofit corporation that the person organized while living.

Since personal contributions to many nonprofit corporations are tax-deductible, many tax-exempt corporations utilize this incentive to obtain substantial funds that often run into the millions of dollars for their operations. Many fundraising firms help nonprofit corporations with fundraising.

Owners of a nonprofit corporation should contact an Internal Revenue office and obtain forms to qualify for tax-exempt status. See IRS booklet No. 557.

Nonstock   Nonprofit

CERTIFICATE OF INCORPORATION
of
__Associated Charities, Inc.__

FIRST: The name of this corporation is _____ Associated Charities, Inc. _____

SECOND. Its registered office in the State of Delaware is to be located at _Three Christina Centre, 201 North Walnut Street_, in the City of _Wilmington_, County of _New Castle_. The registered agent in charge therefore is _The Company Corporation_ at _the same address._

THIRD: The nature of the business and the objects and purposes proposed to be transacted, promoted and carried on are to do any and all the things herein mentioned, as fully and to the same extent as natural persons might or could do, and in any part of the world, vis:

This is a nonstock, nonprofit corporation. The purpose of the corporation is to engage in any lawful act or activity for which nonprofit corporations may be organized under the General Corporation Law of Delaware.

Said corporation is organized exclusively for charitable, religious, educational, and scientific purposes, including, for such purposes, the making of distributions to organizations that qualify as exempt organizations under Section 501(c)(3) of the Internal Revenue Code of 1954 (or the corresponding provision of any future United States Internal Revenue law), to wit:

(In this space you may wish to include a statement describing the purpose and objectives of the corporation in more specific terms.)

FOURTH: The corporation shall not have any capital stock and the conditions of membership shall be stated in the bylaws.

FIFTH: The name and mailing address of the incorporator is: _(leave blank if using The Company Corporation as your registered agent.)_

SIXTH: The powers of the incorporator are to terminate upon filing of the certificate of incorporation, and the name(s) and mailing address(es) of the person(s) who are to serve as director(s) until their successors are elected are as follows:

Kathy Smith, 621 North Street, Anytown, Anystate 00000

SEVENTH: The activities and affairs of the corporation shall be managed by a board of directors. The number of directors which shall constitute the whole board shall be such as from time to time shall be fixed by, or in the manner provided in, the bylaws, but in no case shall the number be less than one. The directors need not be members of the corporation unless so required by the bylaws or by statute. The board of directors shall be elected by the members at the annual meeting of the corporation to be held on such date as the bylaws may provide, and shall hold office until their successors are respectively elected and qualified. The bylaws shall specify the number of directors necessary to constitute a quorum. The board of directors may, by resolution or resolutions passed by a majority of the whole board, designate one or more committees which, to the extent provided in said resolution or resolutions or in the bylaws of the corporation, shall have and may exercise all the powers of the board of directors in the management of the activities and affairs of the corporation. They may further have power to authorize the seal of the corporation to be affixed to all papers which may require it; and such committee or committees shall have such name or names as may be stated in the bylaws of the corporation or as may be determined from time to time by resolution adopted by the board of directors. The directors of the corporation may, if the bylaws so provide, be classified as to term of office. The corporation may elect such officers as the bylaws may specify, subject to the provisions of the statute, who shall have titles and exercise such duties as the bylaws may provide. The board of directors is expressly authorized to make, alter, or repeal the bylaws of this corporation. This corporation may in its bylaws confer powers upon its board of directors in addition to the foregoing, and in addition to the powers and authorities expressly conferred upon them by statute. This is true, provided that the board of directors shall not exercise any power of authority conferred herein or by statute upon the members.

EIGHTH: Meetings of members may be held without the State of Delaware, if the bylaws so provide. The books of the corporation may be kept (subject to any provisions contained in the statutes) outside the State of Delaware at such place or places as may be from time to time designated by the board of directors.

NINTH: No part of the net earnings of the corporation shall inure to the benefit of, or be distributable to, its members, directors, officers or other private persons, except that the corporation shall be authorized and empowered to pay reasonable compensation for services rendered and to make payments and distributions in furtherance of the purposes set forth in article three hereof. No part of the activities of the corporation shall consist of the carrying on of propaganda, or otherwise attempting to intervene in (including the publishing or distribution of statements) any of these articles. The corporation shall not carry on any other activities not permitted to be carried on (a) by a corporation exempt from federal income tax under Section 501(c)(3) of the Internal Revenue Code of 1954 (or the corresponding provision of any future United States Internal Revenue law) or (b) by a corporation, contributions to which are deductible under Section 170(c)(2) of the Internal Revenue Code of 1954 (or the corresponding provision of any future United States Internal Revenue law).

TENTH: Upon the dissolution of the corporation, the board of directors shall, after paying or making provisions for the payment of all of the liabilities of the corporation, dispose of all of the assets of the corporation exclusively for the purpose of the corporation in such manner, or to such organization or organizations and operated exclusively for charitable, educational, religious, or scientific purposes as shall at the time qualify as an exempt organization under Section 501(c)(3) of the Internal Revenue Code of 1954 (or the corresponding provision of any future United States Law) as the board of directors shall determine. Any such assets not so disposed of shall be disposed of by the Court of Common Pleas of the county in which the principal office of the corporation is then located, exclusively for such purposes or to such organization or organizations, as said Court shall determine, which are organized and operated exclusively for such designated purposes.

ELEVENTH: The corporation reserves the right to amend, alter, change or repeal any provision contained in this certificate of incorporation, in the manner now or hereafter prescribed by the statute, and all rights conferred upon members herein are granted subject to their reservation.

TWELFTH: Directors of the corporation shall not be liable to either the corporation or its members for monetary damages for a breach of fiduciary duties unless the breach involves: (1) a director's duty of loyalty to the corporation or its members; (2) acts or omissions not in good faith or which involve intentional misconduct or a knowing violation of law; (3) a transaction from which the director derived an improper personal benefit.

I, THE UNDERSIGNED, being each of the incorporators hereinbefore named, for the purpose of forming a nonprofit corporation pursuant to Chapter 1 of Title 8 of the Delaware Code, do make this certificate, hereby declaring and certifying that the facts herein stated are true, and accordingly have hereunto set my hand this

___14th___ day of _____June_____ A.D. 19_xx_ .

John Doe
_____
(Signature of Incorporator. Leave blank if
The Company Corporation is your registered agent.)

Nonstock   Nonprofit

CERTIFICATE OF INCORPORATION
of
_____

FIRST: The name of this corporation is _____
_____

SECOND: Its registered office in the State of Delaware is to be located at _____
_____ in the City of _____, County of _____
_____. The registered agent in charge thereof is _____
_____ at _____
address.

THIRD: The nature of the business and the objects and purposes proposed to be transacted, promoted and carried on are to do any and all the things herein mentioned, as fully and to the same extent as natural persons might or could do, and in any part of the world, vis:

This is a nonstock, nonprofit corporation. The purpose of the corporation is to engage in any lawful act or activity for which nonprofit corporations may be organized under the General Corporation Law of Delaware.

Said corporation is organized exclusively for charitable, religious, educational, and scientific purposes, including, for such purposes, the making of distributions to organizations that qualify as exempt organizations under Section 501(c)(3) of the Internal Revenue Code of 1954 (or the corresponding provision of any future United States Internal Revenue law), to wit:

FOURTH: The corporation shall not have any capital stock and the conditions of membership shall be stated in the bylaws.

FIFTH: The name and mailing address of the incorporator is:

SIXTH: The powers of the incorporator are to terminate upon filing of the certificate of incorporation, and the name(s) and mailing address(es) of the persons who are to serve as director(s) until their successors are elected are as follows:

SEVENTH: The activities and affairs of the corporation shall be managed by a board of directors. The number of directors which shall constitute the whole board shall be such as from time to time shall be fixed by, or in the manner provided in, the bylaws, but in no case shall the number be less than one. The directors need not be members of the corporation unless so required by the bylaws or by statute. The board of directors shall be elected by the members at the annual meeting of the corporation to be held on such date as the bylaws may provide, and shall hold office until their successors are respectively elected and qualified. The bylaws shall specify the number of directors necessary to constitute a quorum. The board of directors may, by resolution or resolutions passed by a majority of the whole board, designate one or more committees which, to the extent provided in said resolution or resolutions or in the bylaws of the corporation, shall have and may exercise all the powers of the board of directors in the management of the activities and affairs of the corporation. They may further have power to authorize the seal of the corporation to be affixed to all papers which may require it; and such committee or committees shall have such name or names as may be stated in the bylaws of the corporation or as may be determined from time to time by resolution adopted by the board of directors. The directors of the corporation may, if the bylaws so provide, be classified as to term of office. The corporation may elect such officers as the bylaws may specify, subject to the provisions of the statute, who shall have titles and exercise such duties as the bylaws may provide. The board of directors is expressly authorized to make, alter, or repeal the bylaws of this corporation. This corporation may in its bylaws confer powers upon its board of directors in addition to the foregoing, and in addition to the powers and authorities expressly conferred upon them by statute. This is true, provided that the board of directors shall not exercise any power of authority conferred herein or by statute upon the members.

EIGHTH: Meetings of members may be held without the State of Delaware, if the bylaws so provide. The books of the corporation may be kept (subject to any provisions contained in the statutes) outside the State of Delaware at such place or places as may be from time to time designated by the board of directors.

NINTH: No part of the net earnings of the corporation shall inure to the benefit of, or be distributable to, its members, directors, officers or other private persons, except that the corporation shall be authorized and empowered to pay reasonable compensation for services rendered and to make payments and distributions in furtherance of the purposes set forth in article three hereof. No part of the activities of the corporation shall consist of the carrying on of propaganda, or otherwise attempting to intervene in (including the publishing or distribution of statements) any of these articles, the corporation shall not carry on any other activities not permitted to be carried on (a) by a corporation exempt from federal income tax under Section 501(c)(3) of the Internal Revenue Code of 1954 (or the corresponding provision of any future United States Internal Revenue law) or (b) by a corporation, contributions to which are deductible under Section 170(c)(2) of the Internal Revenue Code of 1954 (or the corresponding provision of any future United States Internal Revenue law).

TENTH: Upon the dissolution of the corporation, the board of directors shall, after paying or making provisions for the payment of all of the liabilities of the corporation, dispose of all of the assets of the corporation exclusively for the purpose of the corporation in such manner, or to such organization or organizations and operated exclusively for charitable, educational, religious, or scientific purposes as shall at the time qualify as an exempt organization under Section 501(c)(3) of the Internal Revenue Code of 1954 (or the corresponding provision of any future United States law) as the board of directors shall determine. Any such assets not so disposed of shall be disposed of by the Court of Common Pleas of the county in which the principal office of the corporation is then located, exclusively for such purposes or to such organization or organizations, as said Court shall determine, which are organized and operated exclusively for such designated purposes.

ELEVENTH: The corporation reserves the right to amend, alter, change or repeal any provision contained in this certificate of incorporation, in the manner now or hereafter prescribed by the statute, and all rights conferred upon members herein are granted subject to their reservation.

TWELFTH: Directors of the corporation shall not be liable to either the corporation or its members for monetary damages for a breach of fiduciary duties unless the breach involves: (1) a director's duty of loyalty to the corporation or its members; (2) acts or omissions not in good faith or which involve intentional misconduct or a knowing violation of law; (3) a transaction from which the director derived an improper personal benefit.

I, THE UNDERSIGNED, being each of the incorporators hereinbefore named, for the purpose of forming a nonprofit corporation pursuant to Chapter 1 of Title 8 of the Delaware Code, do make this certificate, hereby declaring and certifying that the facts herein stated are true, and accordingly have hereunto set my hand this

_____ day of _____ A.D. 19____.

_____
(Signature of Incorporator. Leave blank if
The Company Corporation is your registered agent.)

Nonstock   Nonprofit

CERTIFICATE OF INCORPORATION
of

_____

FIRST: The name of this corporation is _____
_____

SECOND: Its registered office in the State of Delaware is to be located at _____
_____ in the City of _____, County of _____
_____. The registered agent in charge thereof is _____
_____ at _____
address.

THIRD: The nature of the business and the objects and purposes proposed to be transacted, promoted and carried on are to do any and all the things herein mentioned, as fully and to the same extent as natural persons might or could do, and in any part of the world, vis:

This is a nonstock, nonprofit corporation. The purpose of the corporation is to engage in any lawful act or activity for which nonprofit corporations may be organized under the General Corporation Law of Delaware.

Said corporation is organized exclusively for charitable, religious, educational, and scientific purposes, including, for such purposes, the making of distributions to organizations that qualify as exempt organizations under Section 501(c)(3) of the Internal Revenue Code of 1954 (or the corresponding provision of any future United States Internal Revenue law), to wit:

FOURTH: The corporation shall not have any capital stock and the conditions of membership shall be stated in the bylaws.

FIFTH: The name and mailing address of the incorporator is:

SIXTH: The powers of the incorporator are to terminate upon filing of the certificate of incorporation, and the name(s) and mailing address(es) of the persons who are to serve as director(s) until their successors are elected are as follows:

SEVENTH: The activities and affairs of the corporation shall be managed by a board of directors. The number of directors which shall constitute the whole board shall be such as from time to time shall be fixed by, or in the manner provided in, the bylaws, but in no case shall the number be less than one. The directors need not be members of the corporation unless so required by the bylaws or by statute. The board of directors shall be elected by the members at the annual meeting of the corporation to be held on such date as the bylaws may provide, and shall hold office until their successors are respectively elected and qualified. The bylaws shall specify the number of directors necessary to constitute a quorum. The board of directors may, by resolution or resolutions passed by a majority of the whole board, designate one or more committees which, to the extent provided in said resolution or resolutions or in the bylaws of the corporation, shall have and may exercise all the powers of the board of directors in the management of the activities and affairs of the corporation. They may further have power to authorize the seal of the corporation to be affixed to all papers which may require it; and such committee or committees shall have such name or names as may be stated in the bylaws of the corporation or as may be determined from time to time by resolution adopted by the board of directors. The directors of the corporation may, if the bylaws so provide, be classified as to term of office. The corporation may elect such officers as the bylaws may specify, subject to the provisions of the statute, who shall have titles and exercise such duties as the bylaws may provide. The board of directors is expressly authorized to make, alter, or repeal the bylaws of this corporation. This corporation may in its bylaws confer powers upon its board of directors in addition to the foregoing, and in addition to the powers and authorities expressly conferred upon them by statute. This is true, provided that the board of directors shall not exercise any power of authority conferred herein or by statute upon the members.

EIGHTH: Meetings of members may be held without the State of Delaware, if the bylaws so provide. The books of the corporation may be kept (subject to any provisions contained in the statutes) outside the State of Delaware at such place or places as may be from time to time designated by the board of directors.

NINTH: No part of the net earnings of the corporation shall inure to the benefit of, or be distributable to, its members, directors, officers or other private persons, except that the corporation shall be authorized and empowered to pay reasonable compensation for services rendered and to make payments and distributions in furtherance of the purposes set forth in article three hereof. No part of the activities of the corporation shall consist of the carrying on of propaganda, or otherwise attempting to intervene in (including the publishing or distribution of statements) any of these articles, the corporation shall not carry on any other activities not permitted to be carried on (a) by a corporation exempt from federal income tax under Section 501(c)(3) of the Internal Revenue Code of 1954 (or the corresponding provision of any future United States Internal Revenue law) or (b) by a corporation, contributions to which are deductible under Section 170(c)(2) of the Internal Revenue Code of 1954 (or the corresponding provision of any future United States Internal Revenue law).

TENTH: Upon the dissolution of the corporation, the board of directors shall, after paying or making provisions for the payment of all of the liabilities of the corporation, dispose of all of the assets of the corporation exclusively for the purpose of the corporation in such manner, or to such organization or organizations and operated exclusively for charitable, educational, religious, or scientific purposes as shall at the time qualify as an exempt organization under Section 501(c)(3) of the Internal Revenue Code of 1954 (or the corresponding provision of any future United States law) as the board of directors shall determine. Any such assets not so disposed of shall be disposed of by the Court of Common Pleas of the county in which the principal office of the corporation is then located, exclusively for such purposes or to such organization or organizations, as said Court shall determine, which are organized and operated exclusively for such designated purposes.

ELEVENTH: The corporation reserves the right to amend, alter, change or repeal any provision contained in this certificate of incorporation, in the manner now or hereafter prescribed by the statute, and all rights conferred upon members herein are granted subject to their reservation.

TWELFTH: Directors of the corporation shall not be liable to either the corporation or its members for monetary damages for a breach of fiduciary duties unless the breach involves: (1) a director's duty of loyalty to the corporation or its members; (2) acts or omissions not in good faith or which involve intentional misconduct or a knowing violation of law; (3) a transaction from which the director derived an improper personal benefit.

I, THE UNDERSIGNED, being each of the incorporators hereinbefore named, for the purpose of forming a nonprofit corporation pursuant to Chapter 1 of Title 8 of the Delaware Code, do make this certificate, hereby declaring and certifying that the facts herein stated are true, and accordingly have hereunto set my hand this

_____ day of _____ A.D. 19_____.

_____

(Signature of Incorporator. Leave blank if
The Company Corporation is your registered agent.)

PROFESSIONAL CORPORATIONS

SECTION XX

Professionals in some areas of the United States may be able to take advantage of the benefits of Delaware corporate laws.

The same form used for a business corporation is also usable by a professional. Professionals should add the initials "P.A." (Professional Association) or "P.C." (Professional Corporation) to the corporate title on the certificate of incorporation (e.g., Jones & Smith, P.A.). Such abbreviations as "Inc." do not appear.

However, such professionals as doctors, dentists, architects, lawyers and the like are treated differently under the law than are business corporations because of the nature of professionals' activities (the term *professional* here means a person providing a service for which a license is required).

In order to assure that corporation status for a professional for tax purposes is not disallowed, the corporation that is engaged in the business of providing a professional service must

1. be owned by professionals in the same field and within the same professional practice (within the same office);

2. make provision by agreement to leave stock to other professionals in the same profession and within the same practice, and have a purchase agreement in the event of death with the same provision;

3. not engage in any other business or activity or in an investment of any kind with a professional in the same practice other than that of providing the primary professional service; and

4. make certain that the professional relationship between the person furnishing the professional service and the person receiving it does not eliminate the personal liability of the professional for misconduct or negligence.

NOTE: Because corporate laws vary greatly from state to state with regard to professionals, it is advisable for the professional to write the Secretary of State in the state where he or she practices to obtain information about any other provisions that should be included in the records of this type of Delaware corporation.

Some states have licensing requirements (particularly for physicians) that do not permit a professional corporation to be formed out of state so that a Delaware professional corporation is possible only for professionals licensed in Delaware. To be completely safe, a professional should request an opinion in writing from a state's licensing department before proceeding with the formation of a Delaware corporation.

FOR ADDITIONAL INFORMATION

SECTION XXI

To obtain a complete copy of Delaware's corporation laws, write to The Company Corporation (Three Christina Centre, 201 N. Walnut Street, Wilmington, Delaware 19801), and send $30, which includes postage and handling. This publication outlines the entire corporation law. The writing is cumbersome, but it is well indexed and contains various kinds of helpful information.

If you wish to make an interesting comparison between the advantages of Delaware's corporation laws and those of any other state, you may write the Secretary of State, c/o Corporation Department of any state, and request information on obtaining a copy of that state's corporation laws.

CORPORATIONS FORMED IN STATES OTHER THAN DELAWARE

SECTION XXII

An existing corporation formed in any state other than Delaware may wish to register to do business in Delaware.

A specimen foreign corporation certificate is on the next page. An official of the foreign corporation (i.e., a corporation in a state other than Delaware) may complete the form. A registered agent in Delaware must be appointed. (The Company Corporation will forward the form to the Secretary of State and act as registered agent for an initial annual fee of $45.) The registered agent then files the form with the Secretary of State, Dover, Delaware. The state tax and fees covering the registration of a foreign corporation are $150. This method applies best when a non-Delaware corporation merely wants to register to do business in Delaware. However, there is a way to obtain all the benefits of Delaware corporate law that this one does not accomplish and that is being favored by more and more corporations, including large as well as one-person or family corporations. The objective of the following method is for an existing corporation to obtain the advantages of Delaware's corporate laws.

Under this second method, when a new Delaware corporation is formed, the non-Delaware corporation is merged into this new one. The Delaware fee for a merger is approximately $150, if both corporations have simple formats and no more stock is issued by the surviving Delaware corporation.

An agreement by the two corporations outlining the terms of their merger that specifies the number of shares of the old corporation to be exchanged for the number of shares of the new corporation is helpful. This agreement becomes part of the new corporation's records. After the agreement is completed, a registered agent can assist in filing the forms with the state.

To take advantage of Delaware law, in almost all cases it pays to form a new Delaware corporation and merge the old one into the new one.

FOREIGN CORPORATION CERTIFICATE

THE UNDERSIGNED, a corporation duly organized and existing under the laws of the State of _____, in accordance with the provisions of Section 371 of Title 8 of the Delaware Code, does hereby certify:

FIRST: That _____ is a corporation duly organized and existing under the laws of the State of _____ and is filing herewith a certificate evidencing its corporate existence.

SECOND: That the name and address of its registered agent in said State of Delaware upon whom service of process may be had is _____

_____

THIRD: That the assets of said corporation are $_____ and that the liabilities thereof are $_____; and that the assets and liabilities indicated are as of a date within six months prior to the filing date of this certificate.

FOURTH: That the business which it proposes to do in the State of Delaware is as follows:

FIFTH: That the business which it proposes to do in the State of Delaware is a business it is authorized to do in the jurisdiction of its incorporation.

IN WITNESS WHEREOF, said corporation has caused this certificate to be signed on its behalf and its corporate seal affixed this _____ day of _____, 19_____.

(CORPORATE SEAL)

_____

_____
President

FOREIGN CORPORATION CERTIFICATE

THE UNDERSIGNED, a corporation duly organized and existing under the laws of the State of _____, in accordance with the provisions of Section 371 of Title 8 of the Delaware Code, does hereby certify:

FIRST: That _____ is a corporation duly organized and existing under the laws of the State of _____ and is filing herewith a certificate evidencing its corporate existence.

SECOND: That the name and address of its registered agent in said State of Delaware upon whom service of process may be had is _____
_____

THIRD: That the assets of said corporation are $_____ and that the liabilities thereof are $_____; and that the assets and liabilities indicated are as of a date within six months prior to the filing date of this certificate.

FOURTH: That the business which it proposes to do in the State of Delaware is as follows:

FIFTH: That the business which it proposes to do in the State of Delaware is a business it is authorized to do in the jurisdiction of its incorporation.

IN WITNESS WHEREOF, said corporation has caused this certificate to be signed on its behalf and its corporate seal affixed this _____ day of _____, 19_____.

(CORPORATE SEAL)

_____

_____
President

MINUTES, BYLAWS, ARTICLES OF INCORPORATION, STANDARD FORMS, REVIEW

SECTION XXIII

On the following pages are all the forms necessary to launch a new corporation. For those who are incorporating but not utilizing the services of a registered agent, this book contains blank forms that may be removed and used. Simply fill in the blanks on these forms. (The only items that are desirable for a corporation to have that are not included in this book are the corporate seal and stock certificates. You can purchase these through a stationery store or through The Company Corporation as a complete bound set of corporate forms.)

Below is the procedure to form a Delaware corporation without the services of a registered agent:

1.   Arrange to obtain a Delaware street mailing address if practical.

2.   File a certificate of incorporation with the Secretary of State in Dover, Delaware.

3.   When the certificate is returned from the Secretary of State, file a copy with the Recorder of Deeds' office, using the Delaware mailing address.

4.   Instead of using the forms supplied by a registered agent, tear out the forms on the following pages.

5.   Fill in the blanks on those forms with appropriate information. Keep these forms with the corporate records. From time to time, keep a record of any meeting the directors have by using these forms and filling in the blanks.

6.   If desirable, buy stock certificates (either printed or unprinted) from a stationery store.

7.   Purchase a corporate seal, which can be purchased at a stationery store.

Listed below are the forms on the following pages:

A.   *Statement by Incorporator(s) of Action Taken in Lieu of Organization Meeting.* This form may be used in all cases and for all types of corporations. Signatures are the same as they appear on the certificate of incorporation.

B.   *Minutes of the First Meeting of the Board of Directors.* Complete and use only if there is more than one director. This form is not needed if the corporation is a close corporation.

C.   *Waiver of Notice of the First Meeting of the Board of Directors.* Complete and use only if there is more than one director.

D.   *Organization Minutes of the Sole Director.* Complete and use only if there is only one director and one person holds all offices. This form is not needed if the corporation is a close corporation.

E.   *Bylaws and Articles of Incorporation.* Complete and use in all cases and keep with the corporate records.

NOTE: *Do not send any of the following forms to your registered agent.*
Keep them with your corporate records.

STATEMENT BY INCORPORATOR(S) OF ACTION TAKEN
IN LIEU OF ORGANIZATION MEETING OF

_____

The undersigned being the incorporator(s) of the corporation makes the following statement of action taken to organize the corporation in lieu of an organization meeting.

Bylaws regulating the conduct of the business and affairs of the corporation were adopted and appended to this statement.

The following persons were appointed directors of the corporation until the first annual meeting of the shareholders or until their successors shall be elected or appointed and shall qualify:

The directors were authorized and directed to issue from time to time the shares of capital stock of the corporation, now or hereafter authorized, wholly or partly for cash, or labor done, or services performed, or for personal property, or real property or leases thereof, received for the use and lawful purposes of the corporation, or for any consideration permitted by law, as in the discretion of the directors may seem for the best interests of the corporation.

_____

_____

_____

The following are to be appended to this statement:

Copy of the Certificate of Incorporation

Bylaws

The STATEMENT BY INCORPORATOR(S) OF ACTION TAKEN IN LIEU OF ORGANIZATION MEETING, together with a copy of the bylaws, which were adopted in said statement, was then presented to the meeting by the secretary.

Thereupon, on motion duly made, seconded and unanimously carried, it was

RESOLVED, that the STATEMENT BY INCORPORATOR(S) OF ACTION TAKEN IN LIEU OF ORGANIZATION MEETING, dated _____ 19____, which has been presented to this meeting, be and hereby is in all respects approved, ratified and confirmed, and further

RESOLVED, that the bylaws in the form adopted by the incorporator(s) in the aforementioned statement be and hereby are adopted as and for the bylaws of this corporation.

The secretary then presented and read to the meeting a copy of the certificate of incorporation of the corporation and reported that on the day of _____ 19____, the original thereof was duly filed in the office of the Secretary of State and that a certified copy thereof was recorded on _____ _____, 19____, in the office of the Recorder of the County of _____.

Upon motion duly made, seconded and carried, said report was adopted, and the secretary was directed to append to these minutes a certified copy of the certificate of incorporation.

The chairman presented and read, article by article, the proposed bylaws for the conduct and regulation of the business and affairs of the corporation.

Upon motion duly made, seconded and carried, they were adopted and in all respects, ratified, confirmed and approved, as and for the bylaws of the corporation. The secretary was directed to cause them to be inserted in the minute book.

The secretary submitted to the meeting a seal proposed for use as the corporate seal of the corporation. Upon motion duly made, seconded and carried, it was

RESOLVED, that the seal now presented at this meeting, an impression of which is directed to be made in the margin of the minute book, be and the same hereby is adopted as the seal of the corporation.

The chairman then suggested that the secretary of the corporation be authorized to procure the necessary books and that the treasurer of the corporation be authorized to pay all expenses and to reimburse all persons for expenses made in connection with the organization of this corporation. After discussion, on motion duly made, seconded and unanimously carried, it was

RESOLVED, that the secretary of this corporation be and hereby is authorized and directed to procure all corporate books, books of account and share certificate books required by the statutes of the State of Delaware or necessary or appropriate in connection with the business of this corporation; and it was further

RESOLVED, that the treasurer of this corporation be and hereby is authorized to pay all charges and expenses incident to or arising out of the organization of this corporation and to reimburse any person who has made any disbursements therefor.

The secretary then presented to the meeting a proposed form of certificates for fully paid and nonassessable shares of stock of this corporation. The chairman directed that the specimen copy of such form of certificate be annexed to the minutes of the meeting. Upon motion duly made, seconded and unanimously carried it was

RESOLVED, that the form of certificate for fully paid and nonassessable shares of stock of this corporation submitted to this meeting, be and hereby is adopted as the certificate to represent fully paid and nonassessable shares of stock and that a specimen of such certificate be annexed to the minutes of the meeting.

MINUTES OF THE FIRST MEETING OF
THE BOARD OF DIRECTORS OF

_____

The first meeting of directors was held at _____
on the _____ day of _____ 19____, at _____ o'clock ____M.

The following were present:

being a quorum and all the directors of the corporation.

One of the directors called the meeting to order. Upon motion duly made, seconded and carried, _____ was duly elected chairman of the meeting, and _____ was duly elected secretary thereof. They accepted their respective offices and proceeded with the discharge of their duties.

A written waiver of notice of this meeting signed by the directors was submitted, read by the secretary and ordered appended to these minutes.

The chairman stated that the election of officers was then in order.

The following were duly nominated and, note having been taken, were unanimously elected officers of the corporation to serve for one year and until their successors are elected and qualified:

President: _____

Vice-President: _____

Secretary: _____

Treasurer: _____

The president and secretary thereupon assumed their respective offices in place and stead of the temporary chairman and the temporary secretary.

WAIVER OF NOTICE OF THE FIRST MEETING OF
THE BOARD OF DIRECTORS OF

_____

We, the undersigned, being all the directors of the above corporation, hereby agree and consent that the first meeting of the board be held on the date and at the time and place stated below for the purpose of electing officers and the transaction thereat of all such other business as may lawfully come before said meeting and hereby waive all notice of the meeting and of any adjournment thereof.

Place of meeting: _____

Date of meeting: _____

Time of meeting: _____

_____
Director

_____
Director

_____
Director

Dated: _____

ORGANIZATION MINUTES OF THE SOLE DIRECTOR OF

_____

      The undersigned, being the sole director of the corporation, organized under the General Corporation Law of Delaware, took the following action to organize the corporation and in furtherance of its business objectives on the date and at the place set forth below:

      A certified copy of the certificate of incorporation filed in the office of the Secretary of State on ____ _____, 19____, and recorded in the office of the Recorder of the County of _____ _____, 19____, was appended to these minutes.

      The office of the corporation was fixed at _____ _____ in the City of _____, State of _____.

      Bylaws regulating the conduct of the business and affairs of the corporation were adopted and appended to these minutes.

      It was decided to issue from time to time all of the authorized shares of the capital stock of the corporation, now or hereafter authorized, wholly or partly for cash, for labor done, or services performed, or for personal property, or real property or leases thereof, received for the use and lawful purposes of the corporation, or for any consideration permitted by law as in the discretion of the director may seem for the best interest of the corporation.

      The following were appointed officers of the corporation to serve for one year and until their successors were appointed or elected and qualified:

President: _____   Secretary: _____

Vice President:_____   Treasurer: _____

      Each officer thereupon assumed the duties of his or her office.

      A written proposal from _____ addressed to the corporation and dated _____ pertaining to the issuance of the shares of the corporation was appended to the minutes.

      The following action was taken upon said proposal:

      RESOLVED, that said proposal or offer be and the same hereby is approved and accepted and that in accordance with the terms thereof, the corporation issue to the offeror(s) or nominee(s) _____ ____ fully paid and nonassessable shares of this corporation, and it is

      RESOLVED, that upon the delivery to the corporation of said assets and the execution and delivery of such proper instruments as may be necessary to transfer and convey the same to the corporation, the officers of this corporation are authorized and directed to execute and deliver the certificates for such shares as are required to be issued and delivered on acceptance of said proposal in accordance with the foregoing.

BYLAWS AND ARTICLES OF INCORPORATION
OF

_____

ARTICLE I—OFFICES

SECTION 1. REGISTERED OFFICE.—The registered office shall be established and maintained at _____ in the County of _____ _____ in the State of Delaware.

SECTION 2. OTHER OFFICES.—The corporation may have other offices, either within or without the State of Delaware, at such place or places as the Board of Directors may from time to time appoint or the business of the corporation may require.

ARTICLE II—MEETING OF SHAREHOLDERS

SECTION 1. ANNUAL MEETINGS.—Annual meetings of shareholders for the election of directors and for such other business as may be stated in the notice of the meeting, shall be held at such place, either within or without the State of Delaware, and at such time and date as the Board of Directors, by resolution, shall determine and as set forth in the notice of the meeting. In the event the Board of Directors fails to so determine the time, date and place of the meeting, the annual meeting of shareholders shall be held at the registered office of the corporation in Delaware on _____.

If the date of the annual meeting shall fall upon a legal holiday, the meeting shall be held on the next succeeding business day. At each annual meeting, the shareholders entitled to vote shall elect a Board of Directors and may transact such other corporate business as shall be stated in the notice of the meeting.

SECTION 2. OTHER MEETINGS.—Meetings of shareholders for any purpose other than the election of directors may be held at such time and place, within or without the State of Delaware, as shall be stated in the notice of the meeting.

SECTION 3. VOTING.—Each shareholder entitled to vote in accordance with the terms and provisions of the Certificate of Incorporation and these bylaws shall be entitled to one vote, in person or by proxy, for each share of stock entitled to vote held by such shareholder, but no proxy shall be voted after three years from its date unless such proxy provides for a longer period. Upon the demand of any shareholder, the vote for directors and upon any question before the meeting shall be by ballot. All elections for directors shall be decided by plurality vote; all other questions shall be decided by majority vote except as otherwise provided by the Certificate of Incorporation or/and laws of the State of Delaware.

SECTION 4. SHAREHOLDER LIST.—The officer who has charge of the stock ledger of the corporation shall at least ten days before each meeting of shareholders prepare a complete alphabetically addressed list of the shareholders entitled to vote at the ensuing election, with the number of shares held by each. Said list shall be open to the examination of any shareholder, for any purpose germane to the meeting, during ordinary business hours, for a period of at least ten days prior to the meeting, either at a place within the city where the meeting is to be held, which place shall be specified in the notice of the meeting, or, if not specified, at the place where the meeting is to be held. The list shall be available for inspection at the meeting.

SECTION 5. QUORUM.—Except as otherwise required by law, by the Certificate of Incorporation or by these bylaws, the presence, in person or by proxy, of shareholders holding a majority of the stock of the corporation entitled to vote shall constitute a meeting, a majority in interest of the shareholders entitled to vote thereat, present in person or by proxy, shall have power to adjourn the meeting from time to time, without notice other than announcement at the meeting, until the requisite amount of stock entitled to vote shall be present. At any such adjourned meeting at which the requisite amount of stock entitled to vote shall be represented, any business may be transacted which might have been transacted at the meeting as originally noticed; but only those shareholders entitled to vote at the meeting as originally noticed shall be entitled to vote at any adjournment or adjournments thereof.

SECTION 6. SPECIAL MEETING.—Special meeting of the shareholders, for any purpose, unless otherwise prescribed by statute or by the Certificate of Incorporation, may be called by the president and shall be called by the president or secretary at the request in writing of a majority of the directors or shareholders entitled to vote. Such request shall state the purpose of the proposed meeting.

SECTION 7. NOTICE OF MEETINGS.—Written notice, stating the place, date and time of the meeting and the general nature of the business to be considered, shall be given to each shareholder entitled to vote thereat at his or her address as it appears on the records of the corporation, not less than ten nor more than fifty days before the date of the meeting.

SECTION 8. BUSINESS TRANSACTED.—No business other than that stated in the notice shall be transacted at any meeting without the unanimous consent of all the shareholders entitled to vote thereat.

SECTION 9. ACTION WITHOUT MEETING.—Except as otherwise provided by the Certificate of Incorporation, whenever the vote of shareholders at a meeting thereof is required or permitted to be taken in connection with any corporate action by any provisions of the statutes or the Certificate of Incorporation or of these bylaws, the meeting and vote of shareholders may be dispensed with if all the shareholders who would have been entitled to vote upon the action if such meeting were held shall consent in writing to such corporate action being taken.

ARTICLE III—DIRECTORS

SECTION 1. NUMBER AND TERM.—The number of directors shall be _____. The directors shall be elected at the annual meeting of shareholders and each director shall be elected to serve until his or her successor shall be elected and shall qualify. The number of directors may not be less than three except that where all the shares of the corporation are owned beneficially and of record by either one or two shareholders, the number of directors may be less than three but not less than the number of shareholders.

SECTION 2. RESIGNATIONS.—Any director, member of a committee or other officer may resign at any time. Such resignation shall be made in writing and shall take effect at the time specified therein, and if no time be specified, at the time of its receipt by the president or secretary. The acceptance of a resignation shall not be necessary to make it effective.

SECTION 3. VACANCIES.—If the office of any director, member of a committee or other officer becomes vacant, the remaining directors in office, though less than a quorum by a majority vote, may appoint any qualified person to fill such vacancy, who shall hold office for the unexpired term and until his or her successor shall be duly chosen.

SECTION 4. REMOVAL.—Any director or directors may be removed either for or without cause at any time by the affirmative vote of the holders of majority of all the shares of stock outstanding and entitled to vote at a special meeting of the shareholders called for the purpose, and the vacancies thus created may be filled at the meeting held for the purpose of removal by the affirmative vote of a majority in interest of the shareholders entitled to vote.

SECTION 5. INCREASE OF NUMBER.—The number of directors may be increased by amendment of these bylaws by the affirmative vote of a majority of the directors, though less than a quorum, or by the affirmative vote of a majority in interest of the shareholders, at the annual meeting or at a special meeting called for that purpose, and by like vote the additional directors may be chosen at such meeting to hold office until the next annual election and until their successors are elected and qualify.

SECTION 6. COMPENSATION.—Directors shall not receive any stated salary for their services as directors or as members of committees, but by resolution of the board a fixed fee and expenses of attendance may be allowed for attendance at each meeting. Nothing herein contained shall be construed to preclude any director from serving the corporation in any other capacity as an officer, agent or otherwise, and receiving compensation thereof.

SECTION 7. ACTION WITHOUT MEETING.—Any action required or permitted to be taken at any meeting of the Board of Directors, or of any committee thereof, may be taken without a meeting if prior to such action a written consent thereto is signed by all members of the board, or of such committee as the case may be, and such written consent is filed with the minutes of proceedings of the board or committee.

ARTICLE IV—OFFICERS

SECTION 1. OFFICERS.—The officers of the corporation shall consist of a president, a treasurer, and a secretary, and shall be elected by the Board of Directors and shall hold office until their successors are elected and qualified. In addition, the Board of Directors may elect a chairman, one or more vice presidents and such assistant secretaries and assistant treasurers as it may deem proper. None of the officers of the corporation need be directors. The officers shall be elected at the first meeting of the Board of Directors after each annual meeting. More than two offices may be held by the same person.

SECTION 2. OTHER OFFICERS AND AGENTS.—The Board of Directors may appoint such officers and agents as it may deem advisable, who shall hold their offices for such terms and shall exercise such power and perform such duties as shall be determined from time to time by the Board of Directors.

SECTION 3. CHAIRMAN.—The chairman of the Board of Directors, if one be elected, shall preside at all meetings of the Board of Directors, and he shall have and perform such other duties as from time to time may be assigned to him by the Board of Directors.

SECTION 4. PRESIDENT.—The president shall be the chief executive officer of the corporation and shall have the general powers and duties of supervision and management usually vested in the office of president of a corporation. He or she shall preside at all meetings of the shareholders if present thereat, and in the absence or nonelection of the chairman of the Board of Directors, at all meetings of the Board of Directors, and shall have general supervision, direction and control of the business of the corporation. Except as the Board of Directors shall authorize the execution thereof in some other manner, he shall execute bonds, mortgages, and other contracts in behalf of the corporation, and shall cause the seal to be affixed to any instrument requiring it, and when so affixed the seal shall be attested by the signature of the secretary or the treasurer or an assistant secretary or an assistant treasurer.

SECTION 5. VICE PRESIDENT.—Each vice president shall have such powers and shall perform such duties as shall be assigned to him by the directors.

SECTION 6. TREASURER.—The treasurer shall have the custody of the corporate funds and securities and shall keep full and accurate account of receipts and disbursements in books belonging to the corporation. He or she shall deposit all moneys and other valuables in the name and to the credit of the corporation in such depositories as may be designated by the Board of Directors.

The treasurer shall disburse the funds of the corporation as may be ordered by the Board of Directors or the president, taking proper vouchers for such disbursements. He or she shall render to the president and Board of Directors at the regular meetings of the Board of Directors, or whenever they may request it, an account of all his or her transactions as treasurer and of the financial condition of the corporation. If required by the Board of Directors, he or she shall give the corporation a bond for the faithful discharge of his or her duties in such amount and with such surety as the board shall prescribe.

SECTION 7. SECRETARY.—The secretary shall give, or cause to be given, notice of all meetings of shareholders and directors, and all other notices required by law or by these bylaws, and in case of his or her absence or refusal or neglect to do so, any such notice may be given by any person thereunto directed by the president, or by the directors, or shareholders, upon whose requisition the meeting is called as provided in these bylaws. He or she shall record all the proceedings of the meetings of the corporation and of directors in a book to be kept for that purpose and shall affix the seal to all instruments requiring it, when authorized by the directors or the president, and attest the same.

SECTION 8. ASSISTANT TREASURERS & ASSISTANT SECRETARIES.—Assistant treasurers and assistant secretaries, if any, shall be elected and shall have such powers and shall perform such duties as shall be assigned to them, respectively, by the directors.

ARTICLE V

SECTION 1. CERTIFICATE OF STOCK.—Every holder of stock in the corporation shall be entitled to have a certificate signed by, or in the name of the corporation by, the chairman or vice chairman of the Board of Directors, or the president or a vice president and the treasurer or an assistant treasurer, or the secretary of the corporation, certifying the number of shares owned by him or her in the corporation. If the corporation shall be authorized to issue more than one class of stock or more than one series of any class, the designations, preferences and relative, participating, optional or other special rights of each class of stock or series thereof, and the qualifications, limitations, or restrictions of such preferences and/or rights shall be set forth in full or summarized on the face or back of the certificate that the corporation shall issue to represent such class or series of stock, provided that, except as otherwise provided in Section 202 of the General Corporation Law of Delaware in lieu of the foregoing requirements, there may be set forth on the face or back of the certificate that the corporation shall issue to represent such class or series of stock, a statement that the corporation will furnish without charge to each shareholder who so requests the powers, designations, preferences and relative, participating, optional or other special rights of each class of stock or series thereof and the qualifications, limitations or restrictions of such preferences and/or rights. Where a certificate is countersigned (1) by a transfer agent other than the corporation or its employee, or (2) by a registrar other than the corporation or its employee, the signatures of such officers may be facsimiles.

SECTION 2. LOST CERTIFICATES.—New certificates of stock may be issued in the place of any certificate therefore issued by the corporation, alleged to have been lost or destroyed, and the directors may, in their discretion, require the owner of the lost or destroyed certificate or his or her legal representatives to give the corporation a bond, in such sum as they may direct, not exceeding double the value of the stock, to indemnify the corporation against it on account of alleged loss of any such new certificate.

SECTION 3. TRANSFER OF SHARES.—The shares of stock of the corporation shall be transferable only upon its books by the holders thereof in person or by their duly authorized attorneys or legal representatives, and upon such transfer the old certificates shall be surrendered to the corporation by the delivery thereof to the person in charge of the stock and transfer books and ledgers, or to such other persons as the directors may designate, by whom they shall be canceled, and new certificates shall thereupon be issued. A record shall be made of each transfer and whenever a transfer shall be made for collateral security, and not absolutely, it shall be so expressed in the entry of the transfer.

SECTION 4. SHAREHOLDERS RECORD DATE.—In order that the corporation may determine the shareholders entitled to notice of or to vote at any meeting of shareholders or any adjournment thereof, or to express consent to corporate action in writing without a meeting, or entitled to receive payment of any dividend or other distribution or allotment of any rights, or entitled to exercise any rights in respect of any change, conversion, or exchange of stock, or for the purpose of any other lawful action, the Board of Directors may fix, in advance, a record date, which shall not be more than sixty nor less than ten days before the day of such meeting, nor more than sixty days prior to any other action. A determination of shareholders of record entitled to notice of or to vote at a meeting of shareholders shall apply to any adjournment of the meeting provided, however, that the Board of Directors may fix a new record date for the adjourned meeting.

SECTION 5. DIVIDENDS.—Subject to the provisions of the Certificate of Incorporation the Board of Directors may, out of funds legally available therefore at any regular or special meeting, declare dividends upon the capital stock of the corporation as and when they deem expedient. Before declaring any dividends there may be set apart out of any funds of the corporation available for dividends, such sum or sums as the directors from time to time in their discretion deem proper working capital or as a reserve fund to meet contingencies or for equalizing dividends or for such other purposes as the directors shall deem conducive to the interests of the corporation.

SECTION 6. SEAL.—The corporate seal shall be circular in form and shall contain the name of the corporation, the year of its creation and the words "CORPORATE SEAL DELAWARE." Said seal may be used by causing it or a facsimile thereof to be impressed or affixed or otherwise reproduced.

SECTION 7. FISCAL YEAR.—The fiscal year of the corporation shall be determined by resolution of the Board of Directors.

SECTION 8. CHECKS.—All checks, drafts, or other orders for the payment of money, notes, or other evidences of indebtedness issued in the name of the corporation shall be signed by officer or officers, agent or agents of the corporation, and in such manner as shall be determined from time to time by resolution of the Board of Directors.

SECTION 9. NOTICE AND WAIVER OF NOTICE.—Whenever any notice is required by these bylaws to be given, personal notice is not meant unless expressly stated, and any notice so required shall be deemed to be sufficient if given by depositing the same in the United States mail, postage prepaid, addressed to the person entitled thereto at his or her address as it appears on the records of the corporation, and such notice shall be deemed to have been given on the day of such mailing. Shareholders not entitled to vote shall not be entitled to receive notice of any meetings except as otherwise provided by statute.

Whenever any notice whatever is required to be given under the provisions of any law, or under the provisions of the Certificate of Incorporation of the corporation or these bylaws, a waiver thereof in writing signed by the person or persons entitled to said notice, whether before or after the time stated therein, shall be deemed proper notice.

ARTICLE VI—AMENDMENTS

These bylaws may be altered and repealed, and bylaws may be made at any annual meeting of the shareholders or at any special meeting thereof if notice thereof is contained in the notice of such special meeting by the affirmative vote of a majority of the stock issued and outstanding or entitled to vote thereat, or by the regular meeting of the Board of Directors, if notice thereof is contained in the notice of such special meeting.

WHAT TO DO WHEN AN EXISTING, ESTABLISHED BUSINESS INCORPORATES

SECTION XXIV

There are some steps involved to transfer the financial records of a nonincorporated business to a corporation.

Below is a guideline to follow when a proprietorship or general partnership becomes a corporation:

1. Arrange to form the corporation. Select a registered agent if you are using one.

2. New books and records should be prepared to reflect the new corporate status and the corporation name.

    a. Decide whether to transfer accounts receivable to the corporation. If accounts receivable are transferred to the corporation, notify customers of the change. This is optional.

    b. Decide whether to transfer accounts payable to the corporation. Again, notify creditors if the change is made.

    c. Decide whether to transfer capital assets to the corporation.

    d. Decide whether to transfer inventory to corporation records.

    e. Decide on the ending date of the corporate year to be used for income-tax-reporting purposes.

    f. Decide whether to notify all company associates and businesses dealt with as well as customers of the new corporate status. This can be done with sales-producing advertising and often at no cost. Newspaper editors will usually provide publicity of this change on the financial page. The owner(s) of the corporation should type and send an announcement to the financial editor of the newspaper where the company's office is located.

3. Order new letterheads reflecting the corporate name.

4. Open a bank account in the name of the corporation.

5. Transfer insurance policies to the corporation.

6. Arrange for any leases or other documents to be changed to reflect the corporation status.

7. Arrange to redo with the new corporation any employment contracts that exist with the old company.

8. If your unincorporated business will transfer its assets to the new corporation, you may have to comply with your state's bulk sales laws. Your lawyer can assist you in determining whether the bulk sales law applies.

It would be helpful to consult with an accountant and, if there are complications with agreements, with a lawyer on handling the above details.

A few of the companies that have already incorporated through this book—
From all 50 states and countries throughout the world

Name	Type of Business
AIDA Group Travel Coordinators & Travel Agents, Inc.	Group and individual travel to the general public
Airspeed Refinishing, Inc.	Custom painting of aircraft and other vehicles
Alaska Book Company	Book sales
Allied Auto International, Ltd.	Services and delivery of foreign vehicles to U.S.
Amazing Diets, Inc.	Publishers
American Armed Forces Association	Fraternal servicemen's organization
The American Society of Child Advocates	Nonprofit society to promote children's rights
Arundel Pool Management, Inc.	Management, opening, closing and maintenance of swimming pools
Balancing Act Corp.	Manufacture of weighing scales
The Balloon Company	Operate a balloon for hire
Better Builders & Remodelers, Inc.	Building and remodeling of residential and commercial buildings
Better Business Maintenance Co.	Janitorial and maintenance services
Bost Farms, Inc.	Farming
Calphil Corp.	Import/export
Chronos, Inc.	Financial planning
Cicero Cheese Manufacturing Corp.	Manufacture of cheese
Cindex Inc.	Computer technical services
Covered Bridge Craft Barn and Garden Centre, Inc.	Retail and wholesale sales of crafts, antiques and plants through garden center
Creative Products, Inc.	Marketing organization
Criminal Justice Associates, Inc.	Consultations to criminal justice schools and agencies
The Cron Corp.	Printing, publishing and management services
Cultural Commercial Exchange, Inc.	Cultural/commercial centers and festival sponsorship
Dakota Nomad, Inc.	Bicycle and cross-country ski retail sales and manufacture of accessories
Denticare of Delaware, Inc.	Prepaid dental healthcare plan
Dexterity Unlimited, Inc.	Retail and wholesale sales and production of handcrafted items
Different Drummer, Inc.	Yacht charter
The Dinky Rink, Inc.	Roller skating
Doug's Aircraft Interiors, Inc.	Aircraft upholstery and accessories
Electron Optics Corp.	Manufacture of surveillance equipment
Energy Independence Now, Inc.	Alternative energy sources
Eunitron, Inc.	Provide investment advisory service (publish a market letter)
European Overseas American, Inc.	Banking abroad, merchant banking
Excelsior International Corp.	Import/export
Fallbrook Ranchers, Inc.	Avocado and josoba nut ranching
Family Name Researchers, Inc.	Researching of surnames, family trees, genealogy, production of armorial bearings, etc.
Finance Corporation for Credit & Commerce	Financial and investment services
Flash Clinic Inc.	Service and repair of electronic flash equipment
Garon Enterprises, Inc.	Numismatics
Golconda Feed & Grain, Inc.	Agricultural products
Green Cargo, Inc.	Diversified sales of plants and accessories
Group Two, Inc.	Educational seminars
The Growing Concern, Inc.	Greenhouses, solar systems
Guardian Protective Coatings, Inc.	Applications and sales of protective coatings
Honey Creek Farm, Inc.	Livestock farming
Hypertension Clinic, Inc.	Medical and health care, and teaching
Imperial Adhesives, Ltd.	Light manufacturing
Infinity's Child, Inc.	Decorating glass

Name	Type of Business
Institute for Neuropsychopharmacologic Research, Inc.	Scientific research
International Development Service Corp.	Export/import trade
International Geophysics, Inc.	Geophysical sales and services
Jetair, Inc.	Dealers in aircraft, flight instruction, and general aviation services
K & B Sink Tops, Inc.	Manufacture sink and countertops
The Lighthouse Repertory Theatre, Inc.	Theatrical productions
Mafia, Inc.	Bumper stickers
Mountain Sales, Inc.	Redwood table sales (handmade)
Music Makers Unlimited, Inc.	Musical services, band and orchestra
Nova Hang Gliders, Inc.	Sales and service of hang gliders and accessories
OMV Corp.	Real estate
Old Worlds Antiques Corp.	Wholesale and retail antiques
PeTaxi, Inc.	Rescue, receiving, air-shipping of pets, pet sitting, escort service for housepets
Pickwick Enterprises Corp.	Fish and chips shop
Pineville Medical Clinic, Inc.	Health and medical service
Plane, Inc.	Transportation
Psychynotics Foundation	Research and teaching of hypnosis, mind control metaphysics, psychic phenomena
R and B Logging, Inc.	Timber logging
Rainsong Institute	Advocacy of efficient energy use
Red Dawn Productions, Inc.	Film production
Reel Creations, Inc.	Music
Regina Careers, Ltd.	Self-training courses for home study
Scientific Resumes, Inc.	Polygraph testing
Seaboard Resources, Inc.	Management consulting and trading
Sign of the Times Corp.	Silk-screened garments
Simmons Industries, Inc.	Design, development, manufacture and sales of poultry processing and related equipment and supplies
Snowcrest Corp.	Horsebreeding and training
Sponsler-Nitrogen-Service, Inc.	Retail—fertilizer, chemicals and apply same
Stock Shot Corp.	Marketing curling and skiing equipment
Tectonics International, Inc.	Architecture, engineering, construction, development, and management services in U.S. and abroad
Texmark Corp.	Act as holding company for retail and wholesale operations of liquor and supermarkets, brewing industry
The Thomas Talin Company	Fragrance
Thor-Bred Health Food Corp.	Health food for thoroughbred horses and other animals
To Have and To Hold Shops, Inc.	Misses sportswear
Transcontinental International, Inc.	Coal and energy products, sales and production
Transprocess Manufacturing Marketing Support Corp.	Business, tax and economy advice
Undersea Life Sciences Corp.	Consulting services for diving/hyperbaric-related industries
Union-Euro-Market, Inc.	Investments
Virginia Pork Corp.	Commercial swine production
Whitehouse Foods, Inc.	Retail grocery store
Woodcat Investments, Inc.	Investments
World Amateur Backgammon Championships, Inc.	Promotion of backgammon and other tournaments
World Backgammon Federation, Inc.	Sanctioning body for backgammon tournaments and official players and promoters organization
World Business Investment, Inc.	Real estate investment, sales and business opportunities
World Cycle, Inc.	Motorcycle repair and sales
Xanthippe Corp.	Investments
Zoii, Inc.	Natural clothing, crafts, etc.

INDEX

NOTES

NOTES

NOTES

NOTES

NOTES

NOTES

NOTES

Start Enjoying Greater Financial Freedom
Triple Your Investment Portfolio
SAVE Thousands on Real Estate as a Buyer or Seller

Personal Finance

The Budget Kit
*Create a Smart Budget That Saves You
Time and Money*

With this multimedia kit:
- Automate your expenses and cash flow
- Save your money for the things that really matter to you.
- Spot your actual spending patterns.
- Stay organized at tax time.
- Start enjoying greater financial freedom

Over 50,000 Copies Sold!

Order No. 1800-1301
$34.95

Judy Lawrence uses her years of experience as a personal financial counselor to show how to organize a personal budget.

Investing

How To Buy Mutual Funds the Smart Way
*Find Out How Easily You Can Buy Mutual Funds
and Earn Profits the Smart Way*

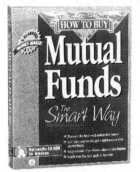

With this multimedia kit:
- Set your own goals and build your lifetime investment program
- Discover an easy way to avoid brokers' fees and reduce your expenses
- Monitor your funds with fully interactive worksheets

Order No. 1800-0701
$34.95

Stephen Littauer has been involved in the sale and marketing of financial and investment products for over 30 years.

Real Estate

The Homebuyer's Kit
Find the Right House Fast

With this multimedia kit:
- Negotiate with confidence
- Prequalify using the automated formulas to determine your best mortgage terms
- Chart your progress using the interactive home comparison forms

Over 50,000 Copies Sold!

Order No. 1800-0401
$34.95

More than 10 million readers watch for **Edith Lank's** award-winning real estate column, "*House Calls*".

The Mortgage Kit
Save Big $$$ When Financing Your Home

With this multimedia kit:
- Select the right loan
- Lock in the best interest rate
- Prequalify using the automated forms and checklists
- Determine how much money you will save when refinancing
- Organize your mortgage search using the interactive checklists

Over 30,000 Copies Sold!

Order No. 1800-2201
$34.95

Thomas C. Steinmetz was a senior strategic planner with the Federal National Mortgage Association.
Phillip Whitt has worked 12 years in residential mortgage lending.

Real Estate

The Homeowner's Kit
*The Homeowner's Kit Will Help You Protect
Your Most Valuable Asset—Your Home!*

With this multimedia kit:
- Save money and conserve energy
- Refinance for the lowest rates

Just point and click to discover:
- Hundreds of home safety and security tips
- How to inspect your home

Order No. 1800-1901
$34.95

Robert de Heer is a professional real estate author who simplifies home-owning with specific money-saving steps.

Small Business

The Business Planning Guide
Plan for Success in Your New Venture

With this multimedia kit:
- Just plug in your financials to plan your dream business
- Point and click to automate planning and financial forecasts
- Start, expand, or buy a business

Over 400,000 Copies Sold!

Order No. 1800-0101
$34.95

David H. Bangs, Jr. is founder of Upstart Publishing Company, Inc.

Successfully Start & Manage a **NEW** Business